CW00435479

The Bishop in Liturgy

An Anglican Symposium on the role and task of the Bishop in the field of Liturgy

edited by Colin Buchanan

Bishop of Aston, diocese of Birmingham

THE ALCUIN CLUB and the GROUP FOR RENEWAL OF WORSHIP (GROW)

The Alcuin Club, which exists to promote the study of Christian liturgy in general and of Anglican liturgy in particular, traditionally published a single volume annually for its members. This ceased in 1986. Similarly, GROW was responsible from 1975 to 1986 for the quarterly 'Grove Liturgical studies'. Since the beginning of 1987 the two have sponsored a Joint Editorial Board to produce quarterly 'Joint Liturgical Studies'. Full details of the separate organizations and of their respective previous publications and of the current series of Joint Liturgical Studies are set out in the end-pages of this Study.

THE COVER PICTURE
is by Peter Ashton—and illustrates the past.

First Impression June 1988
ISSN 0951-2667
ISBN 1 85174 084 8

GROVE BOOKS LIMITED
Bramcote   Nottingham   NG9 3DS

CONTENTS

THE CONTRIBUTORS

John Halliburton is priest in charge of St. Margarets on Thames, Twickenham, London, and was previously Principal of Chichester Theological College. He is the author of *The Authority of a Bishop* (SPCK, 1987).

David Hope is Bishop of Wakefield, and a previous member of the Church of England Liturgical Commission, and was previously Principal of St. Stephen's House, Oxford.

Colin James is Bishop of Winchester, and chairman of the Church of England Liturgical Commission.

David Holeton is Professor of Liturgics at Trinity College, Toronto, a member of the Doctrine and Worship Committee of the Anglican Church in Canada, and Secretary of the first two International Anglican Liturgical Consultations. He is author or contributor to several previous Grove Liturgical Studies and Joint Liturgical Studies, notably *Infant Communion Then and Now* (Grove Liturgical Study no. 27, 1981).

David Stancliffe is Provost of Portsmouth Cathedral, and is a member of the Church of England Liturgical Commission.

Michael Perham is Vicar of Oakdale, Poole, diocese of Salisbury, is a member of the Church of England Liturgical Commission, and was previously chaplain to John V. Taylor when he was Bishop of Winchester. He is the author of several publications on liturgy, notably *Liturgy Pastoral and Parochial* (SPCK, 1984).

'It seems to me that, when a man becomes a bishop in the Church of England, in the matter of the services . . . he is faced with three possible choices. He can trust to luck . . . on each occasion . . . The second choice is that he himself should issue general instructions . . . and should himself supervise the arrangements . . . The third choice is that he should hand the whole business over to some competent person . . .'
> (Robert Mortimer's 'Commendation' in Patrick Ferguson-Davie, *The Bishop in Church* (SPCK, 1961) p.xiii).

'The present volume . . . is an attempt to fill the gap . . . and to give some modest help to new bishops who want to be spared the trouble of having to work out a whole series of ceremonial details for themselves.'
> (Eric Kemp's blurb on outside back-cover of *Episcopal Services* (CLA/Alcuin Club/SPCK, 1980)).

'There is no question that episcopal ornaments at the present time are bedevilled by the use of the staff and mitre. If these could revert to the realms of heraldry, the ceremonies would be unbelievably simplified.'
> (Patrick Ferguson-Davie, *op. cit.*, p.xxxi).

'You will go to church more often than is good for you.'
> (Michael Green, preaching at the consecration of a bishop, 1982).

'I've always reckoned I would have made a good suffragan bishop, going around and blessing organ-stops and what-not.'
> (Anonymous elderly clergyman).

'One of the things that often happens to an archbishop is to find oneself in the middle of a liturgical event without the faintest idea of what is happening.'
> (Stuart Blanch in speech at Design Centre on publication day of the ASB, 10 November 1980).

Introduction

A publication with the title of this one is rare. The famous landmark in Anglican publsihing of this *genre* was the redoubtable *The Bishop in Church* (SPCK, 1961) by Patrick Ferguson-Davie, ceremonial adviser to the then Bishop of Exeter. That particular book was 'based upon the counter-reformed Roman use as laid down in the *Caeremoniale Episcoporum*'.[1] It has thus become a stranded whale on the beach of liturgical history—very weighty, a cause for admiration, but totally non-viable. It is perhaps a comment on trends in Anglican theology also that the S.P.C.K., such a mainstream publisher, should less than thirty years ago have produced such a tome (it has well over 200 pages, and is in hardback) for what must surely have been a limited market?[2] For to the reader to-day the 'stranded whale' effect comes from the following dated features: firstly, from the calm assumption of the author that contemporary Roman Catholic usage is the prime authority; secondly, from the extraordinary detail with which he then implements his programme; and, thirdly, from the inevitable unawareness of the author at the time of writing of the then imminently impending changes in the Roman Catholic Church itself.

Since that great tome appeared, everything has been in much lower key. On the eve of the publication of the ASB, there came out in England a 32-page guide from the Alcuin Club and the Church Literature Association, entitled *Episcopal Services.*[3] This was more modest in style, more contemporary in its programme, more flexible in its advice—but it arguably not only pushed bishops from behind (an inevitable feature of liturgists writing for the episcopate), but also pushed them on the wrong compass-bearing.[6] And the difficulty is that, in a manufacturing industry where the potential market is so small, any one product which purports to meet that market is bound to achieve something near a monopoly.

---

[1] This quotation comes from the blurb on the dust-jacket.

[2] To be accurate, although the publisher was the SPCK, yet the title page gives a further clue 'Published in conjunction with the Church Union'.

[3] The booklet itself reveals its authorship guardedly—it says that it was 'prepared' by Paul Bradshaw and Robert Jennings, 'in collaboration with' Brian Brindley and George Timms. Whether that foursome was the right group for the beginning of the 1980s in England might be questioned.

[4] On the point of 'pushing', one has only to note the style, which is time and again of the form 'The bishop removes his mitre and rises. The book must be held by an attendant . . . For the laying on of hands the bishop sits . . .' (p.19, referring to confirmation). This is insistent beyond the tolerable—and is a good instance also of not only pushing, but pushing in the wrong direction. This is certainly sparing the bishop from thinking (see the quotation from Robert Mortimer on page 6 opposite)—but a moment's thought might deliver him from major and mischievous misdirection.

Other written advice to bishops is thus hard to discover. There are diocesan service books, which may tend to betray the outlook of particular bishops.[1] There is one small Grove Booklet which briefly explores some principles.[2] There is a little coaching in the new Prayer Books of some parts of the Anglican Communion.[3] There is in England a private document of advice which goes out from Lambeth to newly consecrated bishops (and there may well be parallel documents elsewhere). But not only is the commercial market small for any published advice to be given—it is also the case that the bishops themselves, once they have settled into a particular liturgical routine (be it good or bad) usually do not expect to give their minds to questioning it greatly. As like as not each embodies his own view in a set of pastoral regulations, which in turn may have the durability of tablets of stone. If the bishops themselves do not question their own ways, few others in their dioceses will. Furthermore, although the liturgical life of a bishop involves the most amazing round of different kinds of events, the most astonishing requirement of sound principles and a steady nerve, of deep devotion on the one hand and instant responsiveness to unexpected situations on the other—yet no man was ever in this century appointed to the episcopate for his liturgical wisdom or ability, and there exist to this day within the Anglican Communion very few bishops indeed who have made their mark

---

[1] The notable one in England was Leslie Hunter *A Diocesan Service-Book* (Oxford, 1965)—a hardback and thorough, but now rather dated, compilation. This was an attempt to make liturgical provision which could be used anywhere. A more modest, but often substantial, undertaking has been the provision by a bishop, or a diocesan committee, of rites specifically for that particular diocese. A look along a local theological library's shelves revealed three by diocesan bishops:

> Charles Gore *Special Forms of Service for the Diocese of Birmingham* (SPCK, 1908).
> Frederick Ridgeway *Book of Occasional Offices Published for Use in the Diocese of Salisbury* (Brown & Co., Salisbury, 1917).
> Hubert Burge *The Diocesan Service Book Authorized for Use in the Diocese of Oxford* (Mowbray, 1920).

These three are all in hardback, and the latter two are quite weighty. The second, to take but odd examples, includes rites for the 'Re-opening of a Tower' and for the 'Dedication of a Lich Gate'. The third was commissioned by Gore before he resigned as Bishop of Oxford. A recent one was the slightly more home-made (but quite substantial) *Supplement to the Alternative Service Book: Authorized for use in the Diocese of Birmingham* (Birmingham DBF, 1984). The coming of the word-processor has meant that more and more such rites are now stored on disc, and can then be deployed in a host of forms (with hymns and other material added) to meet particular cases—and can be subject to marginal revision each time out, so that a definitive rite is hard to find.

[2] David Cutts *Welcoming the Bishop* (Grove Worship Series no. 88, 1984).

[3] There is a tendency to have sections of the new Books entitled 'Episcopal Services' and some short coaching notes at the beginning of each. See for example the American *Book of Common Prayer* (1979) and the Canadian *Book of Alternative Services* (1985). There is rather more rationale and advice in the 'Prayer Book Studies' which lay behind the American Book—see, for example, no. 20, *The Ordination of Bishops, Priests and Deacons.* (Church Hymnal Corporation, New York, 1970).

as liturgical scholars or as leaders of worship.[1] Men are chosen as prophets, pastors, administrators, diplomats, possibly even as scholars or saints—and *this* one may have been chosen as simply as easy compromise between two opposing strong candidates, and *that* one may have been chosen as simply senior and next in line without respect to merit, and a third may have been chosen for no detectable reason whatsoever. Liturgical knowledge or insightfulness is hardly likely to have been mentioned at any stage.[2] Thus diocesans teach new suffragans odd ways, and the latter in turn become diocesans elsewhere and take the dated oddities with them. At the very least each diocese, or regional group of dioceses, should see vigorous discussions going on between bishops (and with liturgists and parochial practitioners) with an episcopal readiness to learn and to change received ways of doing things.

This particular symposium attempts therefore to do a new thing. The creation of the Joint Editorial Board between the Alcuin Club and the Group for Renewal of Workship (GROW) has led to this new pattern of Liturgical Studies, and, because of the subscription background, such a Study is financially viable, even when of limited scope. The Study is published as the 1988 Lambeth Conference is about to convene, and the Board hopes therefore for the best episcopal market that can be found in one place at one time. And it is published because the Board considered that an open-ended exploration of principles is needed in the Anglican Communion to-day, and is far more needed than is a ceremonial guide designed to give the bishop the 'bottom line' whilst saving him the trouble of thinking too hard.[3] And the hope has been that the Study would touch parishes as well as bishops, and prepare the receivers of episcopal ministry as well as the bestowers of it.

The second international Anglican Consultation on Liturgy met at Brixen in Northern Italy on 24-25 August 1987, following the biennial Congress of *Societas Liturgica*. Papers were read on 'liturgical formation', and most of these have been edited and published as no. 5 in this series of Joint Liturgical Studies.[4] I was asked to read one which is not in that symposium, on 'The Liturgical Ministry of the Bishop'. From that paper the Board discerned the agenda for this Study, and

---

[1] Amongst authors in this century in England one can name Charles Gore, Thomas Drury, Walter Frere (and Colin Dunlop and Henry De Candole among suffragans) and in lesser or indirect ways Frederic Chase, Noel Hudson, Eric Kemp, Graham Leonard, and Richard Rutt. Overseas Donald Robinson, the present Archbishop of Sydney, might be added. The general upshot is to leave the whole House of Bishops both in England and overseas very short of expertise in this vital area.

[2] I have twice recently sat on a Vacancy in See Committee, but in neither vacancy noticed any wish among the participants to mention liturgical knowledge or expertise amongst the *desiderata* being sought. Somehow that is to be taken for granted?

[3] This is written without prejudice to whether such guides get the answers 'right' or 'wrong' (though the editor for one distrusts most such help which has come his way). The thrust of this Study is to urge upon readers the perils of trying to save the bishop from thinking.

[4] Thomas Talley (ed.), *A Kingdom of Priests: Liturgical Formation of the People of God* (Joint Liturgical Study no. 5, 1988).

asked me to edit it. The contributors all have some honoured standing as liturgists, and all in differing ways have stood close to the liturgical ministry of bishops. But their concern has been as much to see and feel the episcopal ministry from the point of view of the worshippers as from that of the bishop himself. There is, as will appear, a range of churchmanship and styles exhibited amongst them, and I myself, as editor, have cheerfully shivered a lance with some details of other contributors' advice in my closing chapter.

It is because it is *principles* which are the agenda here that there is no necessary agreement in detail between chapters, especially where some overlap of subject-matter has given two writers similar ground to consider. Not all contributors have seen each other's work, though one or two have had the chance and have re-touched accordingly. Certainly none must be held accountable for anything except his own work.

Over and above native ignorance (which may be neither total nor uncaring), there are at least three great further difficulties in establishing principles for Anglican bishops. These are:

1. By sheer seniority of age and standing, the episcopate is more likely to represent yesterday's ways of doing things than to-morrow's. That is all the more likely to be the case in a naturally conservative church, or from a liturgically indifferent episcopate—or where liturgical change has all come recently and had passed the particular bishop by in his pre-episcopal days.
2. There is a tremendous difference between different Provinces and different parts of the world—differences of the scarcity value of the bishop, differences of context and the degree of local inculturation, and differences of churchmanship.[1]
3. There is also a tremendous difference between individuals within the episcopate, and liturgy can duly bring out such differences—from the showman on the one hand, to the stuffed museum-piece on the other, and from the nervously anxious who must have it all planned down to the last detail on the one hand to the informal character who horrifies his clergy by playing it all off-the-cuff on the other. It is hard to see how general principles will hold all these together . . .

Three further particularities affect this Study. Firstly, we acknowledge that we are genuinely writing for Anglicans, and out of Anglican liturgical contexts and experience. Secondly, the strong Western European orientation may not give enough scope to Anglicans in Africa, Asia, and South America—though we hope the advice we give will liberate rather than enthrall such. And, thirdly, this is almost the only kind of Anglican book left which can still, with some interim confidence, use the pronoun 'he' for the figure central to the discussion, and simultaneously acknowledge that the 'he' is not intended to be generic (let alone to be propaganda), but is a report of simple Anglican *fact*.

Nevertheless, despite it all, it is principles which we have sought.

---

[1] This last point comes through in that anglo-catholics have always treated the structure, contents, formality and actual conduct of worship as of higher importance than have evangelicals—and have thus tended to set the direction and pace for evangelicals. The latter, neither having strong principles of their own nor giving the subject such a high priority (and often being few and far between as bishops), have tended to provide a paler form of Ferguson-Davie—or, in reaction, to have been somewhat unprincipled.

1. A Historical Perspective

Two thoughts may occur to the new bishop as he surfaces the morning after his consecration. The first is that he has no liturgical home to call his own, no familiar parish church and congregation, no comfortable stall with his own books. He may of course have a private chapel attended by his staff and family. But he is not the normal liturgical president of his cathedral church and has to run the gauntlet of dean and chapter for regular access or is simply 'wheeled on' at the greater festivals and other state occasions. The second worry may be that he has spent more than he can really afford on an extraordinary collection of episcopal 'togs' which he has been told are essential to his liturgical credibility. The ring sits on his bedside table—that makes some sense. The pastoral staff lies in three sections in a wooden case—that too has an unmistakeable symbolism. But why, for goodness sake, three mitres when one would have done? Who on earth dug up that tattered pair of gloves with an Agnus Dei embroidered on each? And was it an anglo-catholic aunt who remembered a high church Scottish bishop pulling on slippers and stockings just before High Mass at a convent and wrote to ask if he would like these too? All this and the purple frog-footman's outfit he now has to wear when everyone else looks tolerably comfortable in white tie and tails. Liturgically, he may think, he was better off as a parish priest.

History, however, like the heart, has its reasons. It also shows that a misunderstanding of the genesis of episcopal ceremonial has in places cast the latter-day bishop into some unnecessary anxiety and privation at the hands of over-zealous MCs and fussy incumbents. To look therefore at the development of the bishop's place in the liturgy may be salutary as well as a guide to modern practice

First then, the bishop is president of the eucharist. Though the New Testament is silent about who is normally to preside at the eucharist, by the beginning of the second century (in Syria at least) Christians were being warned not to take part in any eucharist that was not celebrated by the bishop or at the very least by someone appointed by him.[1] It would be wrong here to assume that the early church had developed the theory that the bishop, in virtue of his consecration, was the only person, by the 'power' invested in him, to celebrate a 'valid' eucharist. The eucharist at Antioch, as in the churches that Ignatius knew intimately, was the affair of the whole Christian community. There is admittedly only one altar and only one bishop; but there are also with the bishop the presbyters and deacons and the regular congregation of the faithful.[2] The bishop, as Ignatius says, represents (sums up in himself) the whole community;[3] he is responsible for them, he has the oversight of pastoral care and teaching. It is for this

---

[1] Ignatius of Antioch, *ad Smyrn.* viii.1.
[2] Ibid. *ad Phil.* iv.
[3] Ibid. *ad Trall.* i.l.; cf. *ad Eph.* i.3.

reason basically that he is the normal president of their assemblies; and his role as liturgical president is linked very closely to his appointment to promote the unity of wholeness (that is what Ignatius means by 'catholicity')[1] of the local church.

This theology and practice worked well when churches were small and mostly urban. But when Christianity spread to the countryside and large churches were built in the suburbs of great cities, the bishop's eucharistic role became more complex. Presbyters were delegated to take care of country and suburban churches. But the bishop, far from being immured in his cathedral church, was frequently the eucharistic president at one or other of his town or country parishes. At Rome for example, in the seventh century (as in Metz in the eighth) the bishop took particular care to visit all his suburban churches in strict rotation.[2] He himself had his own liturgical 'home' at St. John at the Lateran. But on many days, early in the morning, a procession set out from the Lateran palace, the Pope on horseback with what looked like an elaborate retinue of papal retainers, heading for one of the titular churches in the town. A closer look at the procession however reveals that though the Pope understandably had a few of his own officers with him, (the papal vicar, the sacristan and the treasurer) who all rode behind him, in front of him were representatives of the parish he was going to visit (district deacons, sub-deacons, acolytes etc.).[3] The Pope in other words was not a martinette of a bishop, taking his own 'circus' with him in case the local parish did not celebrate the liturgy according to his liking. He was simply going to join a parish family. He would be the president at their eucharist, he would invite them to breakfast afterwards. He was happy to be led into their church, to be told who was to read the scriptures, who to sing the gradual. He is here in no sense a kind of 'sacramental overlord' asserting his rights to celebrate and demanding that all should be done according to his tastes. He comes as the servant of the people to lead them in the community celebration of the eucharist. Further, his presence as president is a sign not simply of his 'care for all the churches' but of the unity of the churches with one another, as one particular ceremony of the Roman rite of this time illustrates.[4] During the celebration, a portion of the eucharistic bread (the *sancta*), reserved from the previous day's eucharist, was brought to the Pope (during the Introit). From this (after the Canon) he broke off a fragment and dropped it into the chalice as a sign that though he presided in many churches, there was only 'one Flesh of Our Lord Jesus Christ, one chalice to unite us in his Blood'[5], one altar and one eucharist. In earlier centuries, Popes had been accustomed to send by messenger a fragment

---

[1] Ibid. *ad Smyrn.* viii.1.

[2] For Rome, see *Ordo Romanus I* ed. and tr. C. Atchley, (Mosting, London 1905); for Metz see Th. Klauser, 'Eine Stationsliste der Metzer Kirche aus dem 8. Jh.' in *Ephemerides Liturgicae* 44, (1930) pp.162-193.

[3] *Ordo Romanus I*, 2, Atchley, pp.118ff.

[4] *Ordo Romanus I*, 8, Atchley p.128. Cf. Atchley's introduction pp.32ff.

[5] Ignatius of Antioch, *ad Phil.* iv.

of the sacramental bread to the suburban churches as a token of the same principle of unity.[1] Without this, the parish eucharist could not begin.[2] Undoubtedly in some cases this was a restraint imposed on potentially rebellious local factions; but by origin it was the sign of the bishop's desire to share in every parish eucharist as the chief minister of the unity of the people of god.

The *Caeremoniale Episcoporum*[3] (the normative instruction on episcopal ceremonial for the western church from the middle ages down to modern times) presumes throughout that the diocesan bishop will always preside in any parish church or chapel he visits, and that the parish clergy on such occasions will revert to being his assistants. There can be no question, that is to say, of 'parking' the bishop on some suitable chair on the north side of the sanctuary while the parish priest celebrates the liturgy in the usual way. The only exceptions to this are when (a) the bishop is not the diocesan and has come e.g. to preach; hence it must never be assumed that because a visitor happens to be in episcopal orders, therefore he must be given the freedom of the altar—the *Caeremoniale* puts such bishops firmly on the 'faldstool' throughout the service.[4] And when the Metropolitan is present, the diocesan takes to the faldstool and invites the archbishop to preside, principally because the archbishop represents the wider unity of all the churches of the province. The theology of Ignatius of Antioch survives throughout. The bishop is not a 'super-priest' whom the parish is lucky to have for a special occasion; his role as president cannot be separated from his role as pastor of all the churches in his care. And it is only in this light that his eucharistic presidency can be seen to have any proper theological foundations.

Equal in importance to the bishop's role as celebrant in his central place in the ministry of the word. In the early church, the bishop (and not the deacon) would read the Gospel at the greater festivals.[5] We still possess large collections of episcopal sermons from the patristic period and it is significant that it was the bishop who undertook the final instruction of the catechumens during Lent and Holy Week.[6] In additon to regular Sunday preaching, bishops would preach on some weekdays throughout their diocese and sometimes deliver courses of sermons outside their jurisdiction altogether, (the whole of Augustine's 'Sermons on the Psalms' for example were delivered in Carthage and not in Hippo). Preaching was a task which bishops considered of the greatest importance.[7] They normally preached seated (with the congregation standing),

---

[1] Innocent I, Ep. 25 *ad Decentium*, MPL XX, 53.

[2] *Liber Pontificalis* (ed. Duchesne). Life of Pope Zephyrinus ad. loc.

[3] In general on the *Caeremoniale Episcoporum* see L. le Vavasseur, *Les Fonctions Pontificales selon le Rit Romain* ed. le R. P. Haegy, (3rd edn. Paris 1904).

[4] 'Faldstool' = 'folding stool', normally a chair without a back, moveable and rarely foldable, but distinct from the bishop's *cathedra* or throne.

[5] Sozomon, *Historia Ecclesiae* VII.19.

[6] As in the catechetical lectures of Cyril of Jerusalem, Theodore of Mopsuestia or Ambrose.

[7] On the bishop as preacher, see M. Pontet, *'L'exégèse de St. Augustin, Prédicate*, (Paris 1944), Ch. Ier.

seem not to have had a prepared text in front of them (a notary at their side recording as much as he could of the sermon). They assumed throughout that it was they *and the congregation* under the guidance of the Holy Spirit who were exploring the meaning of the Holy Scriptures. St. Augustine, for example, considers himself in preaching as the father of a family breaking bread with his children—sharing in other words the gifts of God with them all.[1] He asks for the prayers of the congregation. 'May the Lord help me', he says one Sunday '. . . ask him to come to my aid. Give me your ears and give him your heart'.[2] Clearly the bishop preaches as the pastor whose duty it is to guide the local church into Christian truth and to guard against false teaching (a duty made clear for church leaders as early as the Pastoral Epistles). But he is not as a preacher the 'man with the answers' and carries no book of infallible doctrine to be delivered paragraph by paragraph to the people. He is a fellow-traveller and fellow-explorer, and shares with his people the 'breaking' of the Word of God as much as with them he shares in the breaking of the eucharistic bread.

The seat (*sedes, cathedra*) or throne is here very symbolic. Much has been written about the origin of the bishop's throne which is a feature of all cathedral churches.[3] Some have suggested that, like much episcopal ceremonial and vesture, it has pagan origins, deriving from the time when bishops acted as civil judges and therefore needed a raised throne to act on behalf of the Crown. The first instance, however, in the early church of a bishop having such a throne constructed for himself met with immediate rebuke. Paul of Samosata incurred the wrath of the people of Antioch when he aped civilian privileges in this way, and we must therefore look elsewhere for the origins of the meaning of the episcopal 'cathedra'.[4] Many would see in the bishop's chair the Christianizing of another pagan custom, namely the seating of the teacher or philosopher on a modest chair before his pupils. Early Christian art has examples of God the Father or Christ, seated like the pagan philosophers in such a chair and giving instruction (the Law, the Sermon on the Mount).[5] That the bishop therefore saw himself as a teacher in this tradition is a much more likely explanation of his choice to be seated before his congregation in a place where all could see him. The raising of the throne is by origin purely pragmatic and has nothing as yet to do with the claiming of civil dignities.

The normal place for the bishop's throne in the early church was at the focus of the apse. A bench for the presbyters extended to each side along the semi-circle and the altar stood on the chord of the apse (an arrangement which can still

---

[1] Sermo 95,l.
[2] Sermo 145.
[3] For a balanced account see Th. Klauser, 'Bischöfe auf dem Richterstuhl' in *Jahrbuch für Antike und Christentum*, 5, 1962.
[4] Cf. Eusebius of Caearea, *Historia Ecclesiae* vii., 30-39.
[5] For examples, see A. Graber, *The Beginnings of Christian Art* (ET London 1967). For seated philosophers see pp.55, 128, 131, 144; for God the Father, seated and giving the law to Moses, see p.192; for Christ, seated see pp.69 and 261.

be seen today, for example, in the Norman Norwich Cathedral in England). With the removal of altars to the east end of churches and cathedrals it became the custom to construct monumental episcopal thrones—up many steps with the bishop caged in under a canopy as at Durham or Lincoln (UK)—with the result that the bishop so enthroned is more or less lost to sight and seems to be unrelated to either the celebration of the eucharist or the preaching of the word. The Victorians, alas, followed this example with their dreary wooden constructions, curtained against the winter draughts. Only under the influence of the liturgical movement of the post-war years have bishops recovered the sense (through the re-ordering of churches) that the throne is directly related to presidency and preaching, and is not a personal pew (like Queen Victoria's in St. George's Windsor) where they may enjoy a footwarmer and a measure of privacy.

Preaching and the celebration of the eucharist are of course functions for which the bishop today at least might be considered well prepared in his earlier ministry as deacon and priest. Other ceremonies associated with episcopal office may be less familiar to the new bishop. How to handle a staff and mitre may seem elementary skills to be acquired without delay. But the ceremonial deference, varying from church to church, with which the bishop may be both greeted and treated throughout the liturgy may make the inexperienced at the very least uncomfortable, if not at times profoundly irritated.

Let it be said first that the greater part of the tradition concerning a bishop's bearing and vesture in the public assemblies of the church derives from Roman court ceremonial. It used to be thought that the church developed these ceremonies out of reverence for the episcopal office and its growing importance in society at large. Since the research of Andreas Alföldi[1] into the etiquette of the imperial court and since the studies of Theodor Klauser[2] on the relationship of court ceremonial to that surrounding the fourth century bishop, it has been firmly established that the Christian church simply borrowed the customs of the Empire the moment their bishops were ranked with the 'illustres', a little below the Emperor and above the senatorial class. It seems to have been Constantine who gave them this rank. At the Council of Arles in 314, the bishop of Rome is addressed as 'gloriosissimus' (the highest of the three classes between the emperor and senators), and in 318 (in a law of Constantine) we have the earliest evidence of bishops being appointed to act as judges in civil and not merely ecclesiastical causes.[3] In this way they entered the civil hierarchy and were consequently entitled to civil privileges in dress and the ceremonies attending their public appearances.

To begin with, bishops dressed no differently in church from senior state dignitaries when performing public functions.[4] The Roman senator of the time,

---

[1] A. Alföldi, 'Die Ausgestaltung des monarchisches Zeremoniells am römischen Kaiserhofe' in *Mitteilungen des Deutschen Archäologischen Instituts* (Römische Abteilung), pp.1-171.

[2] T. Klauser, 'Der Ursprung der bischöflichen Insignien und Ehrenrechte', *Bonner Akademische Reden*, 1. (2nd edn. Krefeld 1948).

[3] This important text is in *Codex Theodosianus* 1.27.1.

[4] for a description of Roman dress related to episcopal vestments, see Atchley, *op. cit.* pp.26ff.

for example, wore a *colobium* (a long white garment reaching to the ankles with short sleeves) and a *paenula*, a large cloak, reaching to below the knees with a hole for the head, much like the modern Gothic chasuble. The *colobium* was sometimes held in place by a girdle. A variation on the *colobium* was the *tunica dalmatica*, a similar kind of garment but with wide sleeves and two coloured stripes or *clavi* passing over each shoulder and down to both back and front of the garment. Cold weather sometimes dictated that more than one tunic could be worn under the *paenula*. But in essence, a Christian bishop, like St. Gregory, for example, wore exactly the same clothes as his father (who was a senator) and indeed his mother![1] The one distinguishing mark that developed in the fifth century was the wearing of the *pallium*—a broad scarf or stole—by origin a gift of emperors to their consuls and subsequently (by tradition) from emperors to bishops and from senior bishops (like Gregory) to bishops of their choice (e.g. Augustine of Canterbury).

By the seventh century, when Christianity had spread north of the Alps to the barbarian regions where the inhabitants wore raffish clothes like trousers and boots and shaggy coats with hoods, the bishop stood out from the rest of the assembly when dressed for divine service. Even at Rome (where skirts were still the order of the day in the time of Charlemagne) the bishop changed from his travelling garb into traditional senatorial clothes before celebrating the liturgy.[2] These have now become the more recognizable ecclesiastical garments—the alb (like the former *colobium*) with a girdle and amice (to cover the shoulders) two linen tunics and the *paenula* (or *planeta* or *casula* i.e. chasuble). Over the last of these is placed the *pallium*. The vestments are put on ceremoniously in the sacristy (*secretarium*). Later orders will direct that the place where the bishop should be vested is the Blessed Sacrament Chapel. But it is quite clear that the bishop still vests according to rank and (by now) ecclesiastical custom and that it is he who in time gives his civil privileges to other orders of clergy. Eucharistic vestments, in other words, derive from the bishops' insignia and are the peculiar contribution of the bishops to the liturgy of both East and West.

In the seventeenth century also (in Spain at least) bishops are found with two further insignia—the pastoral staff and the ring.[3] The staff (not as yet shaped like a crook) represents (according to Isidore of Seville) either the bishop's rule or his duty to correct the wayward or his responsibility for supporting the weak. The ring, long since a symbol of betrothal, represents the commitment of the bishop to his church and in time was engraved with a signet or even enclosed relics (like the ring of St. Hugh at Lincoln). Shoes of a ceremonial kind (like those of senators) are worn by bishops (and not others) as early as the fifth century and in later centuries are ceremoniously put on (together with stockings) before the liturgy begins. (After all, a bishop could scarcely march up the aisle in wet and muddy riding boots!) Episcopal gloves appear for the first time in France in the tenth century. They vary from hand coverings of soft material to solid gauntlets and are worn from the beginning of the Mass up to the canon and then after the

[1] See Atchley, *op. cit.* Plate VII, p.28.
[2] *Ordo Romanus I*, 6, Atchley, p.125.
[3] Cf. Isidore of Seville, *De officiis ecclesiastici* 2.5.12.

communion. Several reasons are given for this custom. Some say that gloves were worn to protect the pastoral staff, some suggest that the bishop in northern climates needed to keep his hands warm (though gloves were ordered throughout the year). Like the shoes, however, gloves were a sign of rank and of the dignity of the office (though one honest bishop, Bruno of Segni, being asked why he wore gloves in mid-summer, replied quite simply that they kept his hands clean).[1]

The mitre[1], probably the most distinctive garb of a bishop in the liturgy in recent years, originates in the *camelaucum*, a cap covering the ears worn by the highest dignitaries in Rome under the empire. It is this headgear that gave rise to the western mitre (as the tiara, worn by emperors is the ancestor of eastern bishop's crown). In course of time two three-cornered *cornua* were affixed to the front and back, and a broad ribbon inserted to run round the brim of the cap and then tied at the back in order to tighten it. Hence the 'bands' hanging down behinc the modern mitre. By the twelfth century, mitres were of three kinds— the *pretiosa* (i.e. bejewelled) the *auriphrygiota* (i.e. cloth of gold) and the *simplex* (a plain white)—worn at different seasons and on different occasions. It should be noted that the mitre has nothing to do with the Greek 'mitra' or 'turban' and takes its name from the Septuagint translation of the Pentateuch in whch Aaron (a type of the bishop) is described as wearing a 'mitre'. The mitre came to be worn throughout the liturgy but was removed during the principal prayers (collect, canon and postcommunion).

Mitres and most traditional episcopal vestments ceased to be used in the Church of England at the Reformation, the mitre only being used by the Archbishop of Canterbury at the coronation of the monarch. The alb was retained, developing into what came to be known as the rochet, and a chimere was added (a sleeveless silk or satin gown deriving possibly from the medieval tabard). The cope, so often worn by Anglican bishops today, is not strictly speaking an episcopal garment. It is related to the chasuble (*paenula, pluviale*)and the name 'cappa' first appears in the sixth century. Any cleric could wear it and in the Middle Ages, it became a ceremonial choir habit. Canon 24 of the 1604 canons orders the use of a cope for the celebrant of holy communion in cathedral and collegiate churches. Bishops of the Anglican communion gradually adopted in the nineteenth century the mitre under the influence of the liturgical and ritualist movements of the nineteenth century and today 'cope and mitre' is virtually the norm for the modern bishop, being no longer universally considered a dress specifically related to 'high church' tendencies.

The bishop so often seen in today's church—enthroned, mitred, vested, processed in with lights and incense, genuflected to, attended to for his every need— may seem a far cry from Ignatius of Antioch's pastoral bishop, dressed in lay attire, gathering the persecuted church around him at the altar and preaching to them the word of God. It has to be said, however on the one hand that despite

---

[1] For an account of all these insignia, see the monumental work by J. Braun, *Di liturgiswche Gewandung im Occident und Orient*, (2nd impression, Darmstadt, 1964).
[2] On the mitre, see Th. Klauser, art. 'Mitra' in *Lexikon für Theologie und Kirche* s.v.

the elaboration of ceremonial and the civil dignity conferred on the Christian bishop, theologically his role has never changed and even the most detailed 'ordo's (like the *Caeremoniale Episcoporum*) have been designed to safeguard his role as pastor of all the churches in his care and promoter of their unity. As president of the eucharist, he unites them in the one loaf and the one cup and as preacher of the Word of God he guides them into the way and the truth which all seek to follow for their common wholeness and salvation. Nothing can take away from this.

The significant development however from the fourth century onwards by which the Christian bishop is marked out by his civil rank, his dress and the ceremonial privileges that accompany this (procession, lights, incense etc.) does say something important about the relationship between church and society. The eighth century forger of the document known as *The Donation of Constantine*[1] states that the emperor wishes the bishop of Rome to have the same 'princely power' that belongs to him (the emperor) 'but in a higher degree'. This of course reflects the Carolingian theory of church and state whereby Pope and Emperor ruled temporal and spiritual orders side by side under the governance of God, with the Pope, if anything having the edge on the Emperor. But the decision of a State that chose to support the Christian religion to promote church leaders to such high civil dignities does suggest that the Christian religion was considered not simply an allegiance for the committed few, but a spiritual force for the good of society as a whole. In Christian Europe (as in its extension in the Americas and elsewhere) this vision of Christianity being a leaven in society and 'a light to the Gentiles' has never really been lost. And it is perhaps worth the bishop's reflection, as he heaves on his cope (or chasuble), struggles with his mitre, and makes sure his chaplain has his pastoral staff, that entering the Christian liturgy, dressed as a civil dignitary of old, he is, (whether the full force of the symbolism is recognized or not), representing the trust of society as a whole in his own spiritual wisdom and the expectations they have of the church universal. That he should act as he does and be dressed as he is for the liturgy where he is to perform his service under the Word of God at lectern, pulpit and altar must in some sense be seen as symbolic of the bringing of the entire human concern to the heart of the Word made flesh (as the prayers of the liturgy so amply express). The bishop, like the church which he serves and represents, exists for the sake of the world; and it is this that his liturgical role and the rites and insignia that accompany it are designed to express.

2. Past and Present—
The Bishop as Focus of Unity

The use of the phrase 'focus of unity' as descriptive of the work and office of a bishop in the Church of God is both new and old. It is new in the sense that this is a phrase which has emerged in a particular way through a variety of contemporary ecumenical dialogues and can perhaps best be typified by a sentence from The 'Lima' Statement: 'They [bishops] provide a focus for unity in life and witness within areas comprising several eucharistic communities.'[1] It is old in the sense that from the very beginning a key aspect of the ministry of the bishop has been that he acts as a visible and tangible centre of unity among the communities which comprise his 'diocese'.

For the Christian group or community the source of all unity must be God himself. He is the fount and origin of all that is—all things were created by him and it is in him that everything has its being and its final fulfilment. The world, as we experience for ourselves so often, is a world fractured by sin, where there is division and alienation which can and does run deep, and which seems to persist even in spite of our best efforts. The unswerving assertion of the New Testament is that God was in Christ reconciling the world to himself, restoring unity to the whole human race. This 'salvation' was effected for all, in and through Christ's once-for-all death upon the cross and his mighty triumph over death in his resurrection and the outpouring of the Holy Spirit. In this act of God in Christ, the possibility is opened up and offered of forgiveness of sin and restoration to newness of life in harmony with God and with each other. It is this saving work of God shown forth in the death and resurrection of Jesus which is the way to unity for the whole human race. This is the good news—'Repent, and believe the gospel'—which is at the heart of the New Testament proclamation.

GOSPEL AND CHURCH

But the gospel cannot remain something purely abstract or theoretical, nor is it to be proclaimed in the realm of the 'spiritual' alone. Further, gospel and church must go hand in hand, for the two emerge together as part of that new humanity, a new creation, a new community which was now in the process of being fashioned through the Lord's death and resurrection. It is the consistent teaching of the New Testament, and of Paul in particular that as Christ was the 'sacrament' of God among us, so the Church is the 'sacrament' of Christ, and, to continue the language of sacramental theology, it effects what it signifies. Thus the church, the Christian community, visible, fallible, tangible and vulnerable, yet filled with the mighty power of God's Spirit, is the means by which Jesus Christ would draw all mankind into unity with God. And it must surely follow that all

---

[1] *Baptism, Eucharist and Ministry* (Faith and Order Paper no. 111, WCC, 1982) p.24.

and every authentic ministry in the church must be at the service of this sanctifying and saving work. It is to be an outward and visible sign of the work of Christ in the power of the Spirit as he continues to uphold and sustain, guide and direct the work of his church, through which he would draw all people into unity with himself: in some words of Cyprian of Carthage on the Unity of the Church:

'the unity of the Godhead, of the person of Christ, of the ideal church, of the faith, must be reproduced in the unity of the earthly congregation . . . the unity of humanity, within itself and with God is that in which alone salvation consists'.

So, fundamental to the work and office of a bishop is that he keeps the body of Christ, the church, faithful to its real and primary task, namely the building up of the unity which is given us in the crucified and risen Lord.

BISHOP AND UNITY

It is this theme of the creation of unity through the building up of the Christian community in self-giving love which is an underlying and constant element where much else is imprecise and untidy as Church order begins to emerge in the New Testament. The earliest days were clearly days of diversity and discovery. There were still those who had received a direct commission from the risen Lord, and were exercising as apostles an itinerant ministry. It could be said that always their priority was to build up, to weld into unity, the new communities of Christian believers. To that extent, from the very beginning 'episcope' was a feature of such a ministry and it was exercised in obedience to a higher authority—that of Jesus Christ himself. It was a call and a charge given by Christ quite without regard for status, learning, human ability or anything else. Further, it was a direct and head-on challenge to that self-aggrandisement which is so often to be found in those who exercise power and authority in the kingdoms of this world, for here was a power and authority in the service of the gospel of the Lord Jesus Christ.

It is difficult to discern in the emerging church and the establishing of its worder any clear and consistent pattern of development. Along with the itinerant apostles, the New Testament seems to indicate that there were other ministries being exercised locally, and among them those of the presbyter-bishops and that of the deacons, each with different functions. During this time, and indeed for some time to come, the 'bishop' and 'presbyter' were interchangeable and referred to the same ministry. Only slowly did the threefold pattern emerge with one bishop to each local church, assisted by presbyters and deacons. It may be surmised that, during the second century, with the Apostolic Tradition of Hippolytus in mind, in larger towns and cities like Rome and Antioch the presbyters came to exercise a more distinct ministry. Indeed they are a second order of ministry but closely connected to that of the bishop, and this is very evident from the form of prayer used at their ordination, as it is set out in the Apostolic Tradition of Hippolytus, in many ways like the ASB form of ordination, virtually the same prayer, except in certain particulars. In the prayer at the ordination of a presbyter in Hippolytus, the presbyters are compared to the elders appointed by Moses in the Old Testament as the burden of doing everything himself became too heavy to bear. The presbyter then is the local 'bishop' and is empowered to exercise precisely the same ministry except to ordain. When the bishop visits his local church, the presbyter yields his place to the bishop as the one president of the eucharistic assembly; in very much the same way as happens in our own day when a bishop makes his parish visit. Gregory Dix comments:

'The presbyter has no peculiar liturgical office in the presence of the bishop, who is the ordinary sacramental minister of his own Church, assisted by the deacons. But in the absence of the bishop the presbyter can act as his liturgical deputy and perform his sacramental functions assisted by the deacons'.[1]

The ministry was one ministry (the bishop was also a presbyter and could be referred to as such: similarly he would often address his fellow presbyters as co-presbyters) and all ministry was and continued to be exercised in union with the bishop. This was further demonstrated by the presbyters joining together with the bishop in the ordination of a presbyter, thus showing in an outward and visible way that unity in Christ which all share in their ministerial office in the church, as on those occasions also when the presbyters would join with the bishop in his celebration of the Eucharist.

Thus the unity to which God calls all people in Christ through the church is a theme which, established in the gospel itself, becomes an essential element in the order of the church as it emerges into the threefold elements of bishop, presbyter and deacon. And in this church order the bishop has a key role and a controlling role, so to speak, in the building up and maintaining in communion of the various Christian communities united to him and with him. Already, it has been noted that this key role has again come to the fore in more recent times as the churches together seek to express how they understand the term 'bishop', and it has become clear that the phrase 'focus of unity' as used in relation to the bishop in the church is of the very 'esse' of his distinctive ministry.

It may perhaps be helpful now to move on and examine three particular facets of how the bishop came to be understood as a focus of unity in the early church, with the emergence and clarification of his role and function, and further how these three particular facets—the bishop as centre of unity in the local church; the bishop as a focus of the continuing apostolic teaching and mission; the bishop as the link person between the local eucharistic gathering and the community of the church universal—how all three have again emerged as very relevant in contemporary discussion on the nature of the episcopate and the exercise of episcope. These three facets did not spring from any purely juridical or administrative concern, but from that which is constitutive of any episcopal ministry in any place, at any time, namely the sacramental and liturgical expression of this particular ministry. Three of the early writers—Ignatius, Irenaeus and Cyprian—spell our in their own way these three distinctive apsects of the bishop as 'focus of unity', and the writings of all three seem to have been of particular significance to Anglican writers and thinkers in their appeal to 'ancient Authors', and it is to a brief consideration of each of these that we must now turn.

---

[1] G. Dix in K. E. Kirk (ed.) *The Apostolic Ministry* (Hodder and Stoughton, 1946) p.220.

It is in his role as president of the eucharist that the bishop is most clearly perceived as the focus of unity for the local church. And the first person really to spell this out and to witness to this fact is Ignatius, Bishop of Antioch, in the post-apostolic age. For him the word 'church' is synonymous with 'eucharistic community', and it is the bishop who presides over this one eucharist. The basic thrust of his message is well summed up in his own words;

> 'Be careful, then, to observe a single Eucharist. For there is one flesh of our Lord, Jesus Christ, and one cup of his blood that makes us one, and one altar, just as there is one bishop along with the presbytery and the deacons, my fellow slaves.'[1]

Very movingly in his letter to Polycarp of Smryna he writes; 'Watch over unity... for there is nothing more important than this.' Nor is a bishop a lordly autocratic kind of figure; the unity which typifies the Christian community is a unity in the love of Jesus Christ, a love which found expression in the sacrificial death upon the cross. So the bishop is bound to and with his people and his people with him—together, bishop, presbyters and people are open to God to be built up in unity and the celebration of the eucharist together is the sacramental sign both of what is to be and what is presently being effected in the church. Ignatius then draws out that feature which remains an essential element in any episcopal ministry—that of binding together and building up in one communion the multiplicity and diversity of the local churches.

IRENAEUS

It is in the late second century that Irenaeus of Lyons draws out another important aspect of the bishop as a minister of unity. Whilst he was quite clearly in accord with the Ignatian view of the bishop as a focus of eucharistic unity, his conflicts with the Gnostics led him to stress much more forcefully the fact that it was the bishop who kept the local church true to the apostolic and foundational teaching. The Gnostics claimed that they had secret knowledge, *gnosis*, a secret tradition handed down by their own teachers. Over against such secrecy, Ignatius argued that the orthodox Christian faith, based on the scriptures, was open and public and it was focussed in the succession of bishops exercising the ministry of teaching and preaching the same apostolic faith, that faith which was consonant with that preached and taught by the apostles themselves. Consecration to the episcopate, with the participation of other bishops, was not an empty ceremony. Rather the presence of such other bishops as could be present was a sign that in the person so consecrated they recognized faithfulness to the continuity in teaching and preaching; consecration was, further, prayer on the part of the whole gathered community that the person so chosen and consecrated would by granted the 'charismata' in order to enable him to continue the apostolic teaching and preaching.[2]

---

[1] Ignatius, *Phil.* 4—cf. John Halliburton in chapter 1 above, pp.11-12.

[2] Such a consecration of a bishop is not actually reported until it becomes the starting point of Hippolytus—but the action described there coheres closely with the rationale of Irenaeus.

Moreover the bishop's credentials could be checked by open examination and inspection. Irenaeus mentions a 'succession list' which was a list of names of the present bishop's predecessors in the see, reaching back to the original apostolic foundation. What is involved in citing this list is not a catalogue of names for the sake of it, but, rather, a way of establishing the genuineness of the present bishop's teaching, bearing in mind that he is the latest link in the chain of such teaching, stemming from its apostolic origins. In Irenaeus', writing about the see of Rome, he appears to have some such document in mind.[1] And it is on this precise point that he challenges the Gnostics:

'Let them therefore produce the pedigrees of their churches, let them unfold the succession lists of their bishops, which should so descend from the beginning that the first bishop, whoever he is, should have as originator and predecessor somebody from among the apostles or the men who are only apostolic but still will have continually associated with the apostles.'[2]

R. P. C. Hanson comments:

'Apostolic doctrines today (as in Irenaeus' time) should mean, not the doctrine taught by the men who are successors of the apostles, whatever they teach, but the doctrine of the essentially apostolic book, the New Testament'.[3]

Apostolic succession then was not so much the tactile succession of the laying on of hands, as an affirmation that in a person chosen to exercise the office of a bishop, continuity in the apostolic succession of teaching and preaching had been recognized. It is also in this sense that the enthronement of the bishop is properly to be understood and interpreted. Thus the bishop is the sign of the unity of this particular community of churches here and now, those which comprise his 'diocese', with the church down the ages, the link with the original foundation of the apostolic faith, teaching, witness and mission.

CYPRIAN

Another important aspect of the bishop as focus of unity, one which will be particularly to the fore in this year as bishops gather from around the Anglican Communion for the Lambeth Conference, is the concept first developed to any great extent by Bishop Cyprian of Carthage in the third century—that the bishop is the link locally with the universality of the churches. Cyprian's distinctive contribution was an exploration of the conciliar and collegial character of the universal episcopate and the way in which the various churches, in meeting together through their bishops (each bishop bringing his diocese with him, so to speak) might work towards a common mind and solve disputed questions and issues. It was Cyprian also who was quite clear that the church catholic was to be found in all its fullness equally in the gathering in any one of its constituent parts, in the local eucharistic communities just as much as in the gatherings of bishops and synods. There could be no question of a supra-world-wide church organization.

---

[1] cf. *Adv. Haer.* 3.3.2.3.
[2] *De Praeser, Haer,* 32.1,
[3] R. P. C. Hanson, *Tradition in the Early Church* (London, 1962).

And so far as the bishop was concerned Cyprian expresses himself thus:

'The church is the people united to the priest, the flock clinging to its shepherd. From this you should know that the bishop is in the church and the church in the bishop.'[1]

So it is through the bishop that the faith and life and experience of a particular local church is gathered up and brought to the wider councils of bishops. The bishop in such gatherings represents communities which are complete in themselves, communities which, in spite of their differing and often somewhat diverse situations and outlooks, bear a family likeness to each other. They meet together to discover a common mind, to become more obedient to Jesus Christ, and better able to represent him in the world in the task of evangelization. There is thus, again in Cyprian's words, 'One episcopate in which each individual bishop has a share and the whole'. In other words the local church is a microcosm of the universal.

THROUGHOUT ALL AGES

The highlighting then of these three writers is not by way of an exercise in patristic antiquarianism, but rather to draw out the three major strands which, having become apparent and established at an early stage, and to a greater or lesser extent having persisted throughout in the work and office of a bishop, are of particular relevance as the bishops of the Anglican Communion come together for Lambeth 1988. They arise from the fact that the bishop is *the* pastor among the pastors who exercise their ministry at his direction, by his authority and with his licence; from the fact that the bishop, in the name of Christ in his church, ordains them and sends them forth in the Lord's name; from the fact that the bishop presides over *one* eucharistic community—that community of the new creation, who not only with their lips but in their lives, offer a sacrifice of praise and thanksgiving together with angels and archangels and the whole company of heaven. So the eucharistic liturgy itself is the point both of departure and return for the bishop as *the* president of that communion of local churches bound together and built us for mission through his ministry. It is this 'communion of local churches' which each bishop will be bringing with him to Lambeth, where they will become one with the universality of all the churches of the Anglican Communion

The central place then which the bishop occupies in the liturgy is not a purely decorative one, it is both symbolic and sacramental—symbolic of the united proclamation of and witness to our common faith in the world; sacramental in the sense that already in the church's worship that unity which Christ wills for all humanity is already in the process of being established—a sign of the final destiny, that freedom and liberation in Christ from all that divides us, as we are born again into new and unending life in him.

---

[1] Cyprian, *Epp.* 66.8.

3. The Bishop Leading His Diocese

1.INTRODUCTION: THE CHANGING PLACE OF THE BISHOP IN LITURGY
Over the past few years Anglican provinces have produced new liturgical texts which give a prominence to the liturgical ministry of bishops which was unknown in the Prayer Book tradition of the sixteenth century. The Tudor Prayer Books, and their successors into this century, assume that the bishop is normatively absent and uninvolved in the liturgical life of the Christian community. Here the Prayer Book liturgical texts were faithful inheritors of their mediaeval precursors: the bishop's book (the Pontifical) had ceased to contain any of the rites seen by the average Christian, while the priest's books (the Missal and the Ritual) assumed that the priest is the normal minister of the sacraments of baptism and the eucharist, the mainstay of the Christian life. The liturgical ministry of bishops was seen as being restricted to confirmation (a rite so ignored that it often appeared in the Pontifical immediately before the ordination rites because so few candidates for ordination had been confirmed) and ordination. When the bishop presided at the sacramental rites, he was seen to do so as a priest rather than as bishop.

In the Prayer Book ordinal the language of liturgical responsibility is absent from the consecration of bishops: exhortations to participate in the liturgical life of the Christian community are reserved for the ordination of priests and deacons. The first mention of liturgical responsibility for bishops does not appear in the English ordinals until 1662 when the bishop-elect is asked:

Will you be faithful in ordaining, sending, or laying hands upon others?

Here the question is more juridical than it is liturgical, in that it is an attempt to emphasize the prerogative of a recently restored episcopate in re-ordering the presbyterian clergy who had come to hold benefices during the Commonwealth and to coerce them into conformity with the re-established Church of England.

It is not surprising, then, that the Prayer Book rubrics in both the baptismal and eucharistic rites pay little attention to the liturgical ministry of bishops. At baptism the bishop is mentioned only in the duties of parents and godparents as the person to whom the child must eventually be presented in order to be confirmed. In the case of an adult baptism the candidate's name must be reported to the bishop (not out of any concern for pastoral care or even for confirmation, but so that a record could be kept of dissenters brought to conformity—just as recusants who communicated also had to be reported to the bishop). In the eucharist the bishop is allowed to absolve and bless as well as receive the names of those who had been repelled from the Lord's Table. There is no rubrical suggestion that he should ever preside at it except in the case of ordinations.

The liturgical texts of the recent past have radically reversed that situation. Liturgical activity is made a primary mandate of bishops at their ordination:

'He is to baptize and confirm, to preside at the Holy Communion, and to lead the offering of prayer and praise.'

(Church of England, *Alternative Service Book*, p.389).[1]

'You are called to guard the faith, unity and discipline of the Church; to celebrate and to provide for the administration of the sacraments of the new covenant; or ordain priests and deacons and to join in ordaining bishops...'

(United States, *Book of Common Prayer*, p.517)

'There is one great High Priest of the new covenant, in whose name a bishop presides over the church's offering and calls all to be of one mind and purpose, that in unity they may present to the Father a single, holy, living sacrifice.'

(*Scottish Ordinal 1984*, p.2)

The prayers of consecration used for bishops now make particular reference to the liturgical ministry of bishops:

'Guide and direct him in presiding at the worship of your people.'

(Canada, *Book of Alternative Services*, p.639)

'Give N authority
to shepherd your flock;
in the name of Christ the one High Priest,
to offer the gifts of your holy church;
to forgive sins as you command,
to order ministries as you direct . . .'

(*Scottish Ordinal 1984*, p.6)

Finally, in the rubrics for particular rites, the liturgical ministries to be exercised by a bishop are now clearly delineated:

'As chief liturgical officer it is the bishop's prerogative to preside at the Lord's Table and to preach the gospel.'

(Canada, *Book of Alternative Services*, p.183)

'The bishop, when present, is the celebrant; and is expected to preach the Word and preside at Baptism and the Eucharist. At Baptism, the bishop officiates at the Presentation and Examination of the Candidates; says the Thanksgiving over the Water; [consecrates the Chrism;] reads the prayer, "Heavenly Father, we thank you that by water and the Holy Spirit;" and officiates at what follows.'

(United States, *Book of Common Prayer*, p.298)

There is, then, little doubt that the understanding of the liturgical role to be exercised by bishops has shifted considerably since the first prayer books. A ministry which normatively was assumed to be juridical and exercised from a distance is

---

[1] In this essay I have drawn on liturgical texts from several provinces. I am sure that they will evoke in the minds of readers parallel texts from other provincial liturgies.

now expected to be pastoral and proximate. The liturgical texts assume that bishops will be a regular part of parochial life and, when present, will not be relegated to the 'bishop's chair' and merely be 'allowed' to confirm, but that they will preach the gospel, baptize, and preside at the eucharist showing clearly whose ministry it is and that the incumbent exercises these ministries on an ongoing basis not as an inherent right but, rather, in the bishop's stead and as the bishop's personal delegate. Bishops ought to feel more secure in the liturgical life of the church than they have at any time since the reformation. This, however, often seems to be anything but the case and is a question that we must now address.

2. THE BISHOP IN LITURGY: A SHARED MINISTRY
(i) LITURGICAL FORMATION

In a number of the new ordinals (Canada, Scotland, the United States) the bishop-elect is asked:

'As chief priest and pastor, will you encourage and support all the baptized in their gifts and ministries, nourish them out of the riches of God's grace, pray for them and celebrate with them the sacraments of our redemption?'

Episcopal ministry is exercised in the midst of the whole People of God and not from without. This has very particular implications for the liturgical ministry of bishops both in the *episkope* of the creation of the liturgical texts and in the actual celebration of those rites with the assembled community.

When the Second Vatican Council published its *Constitution on the Sacred Liturgy,* the document which was to provide the principal impetus for the renewal of Roman Catholic worship, the Council fathers found themselves obliged to speak about the teaching of liturgy:

Professors who are appointed to teach liturgy in seminaries, religious houses of studies, and theological faculties must be properly trained for their work in institutes which specialize in this subject.

The study of sacred liturgy is to be ranked among the compulsory and major courses in seminaries and religious houses of studies. In theolgoical faculties it is to rank among the principal courses. It is to be taught under its theological, historical, spiritual, pastoral and juridical aspects. In addition, those who teach other subjects, especially dogmatic theology, sacred scripture, spiritual and pastoral theology, should—each of them submitting to the exigencies of their own discipline—expound the mystery of Christ and the history of salvation in a manner that will clearly set forth the connection between their subjects and the liturgy, and the unity which underlies all priestly training.'[1]

Now that we as a Communion move further and further from a monochromatic use of 1662 (and quite rightly so) and begin to create more and more Provincial liturgies, we need to pay particular heed to the situation in which Rome found herself on the eve of liturgical renewal. As Anglicans the liturgy is

---

[1] *Constitution on the Sacred Liturgy* I, ii, 15, 16.

central to our common life. That has been repeatedly acknowledged by Lambeth Conferences and the meetings of Primates. The collected papers of the Second Anglican Liturgical Consultation (Alcuin/GROW Liturgical Study No. 5) highlight the diverse ways in which the liturgy forms and nurtures our tradition. Yet liturgical formation is in a very tenuous state throughout much of the Communion. Of those who are asked to teach liturgy in our theological colleges only a minority have made liturgy their principal field of study. Far too often the responsibility for teaching liturgy is given to church historians whose interest in liturgy is more archaeological than pastoral, or to those who teach pastoralia and who see liturgy as merely a matter of how to 'take services' with little reflection on their theological content or historical background.

While not every theological college has the economic resources to permit a faculty member to devote his or her entire time to teaching liturgy, much more care must be given to assuring that those who are called on to teach in this area have the proper academic qualifications for the responsibility entrusted to them. In most Anglican provinces these initial academic resources will not be available locally. Much of the weight will fall on bishops both for choosing candidates suitable for academic study in liturgy and in discovering places where liturgical study can take place. Seeing that the course of study provides sufficient theological, historical and pastoral grounding will be of great importance as will the assurance that their candidates will return home informed by their studies, not limited by them, so that they will be useful resources in creating liturgical texts that will meet the needs of the local Christian community being informed by, rather than bound to, inherited liturgical models. The ability to communicate this to theological students, clergy and lay people will be of paramount importance. This is particularly the case where the liturgy has been a principal way of holding onto the colonial past or where fidelity to both the Prayer Book brought by the missionaries (some of whom may still be a living memory) and the manner in which they used it (and the music they sang with it) have come to be closely associated with fidelity to the Anglican tradition itself. The first need, then, in the shared liturgical ministry of bishops is the need to find candidates for advanced liturgical studies so that the general level of liturgical literacy might be increased in both our colleges and parishes.

When a province has persons who have received specialized liturgical training bishops need to learn to use them collaboratively. Very few bishops are prepared to make theological or ethical statements without first consulting someone with special formation in theology or ethics. Liturgical matters seem often to be in a quite different realm. Bishops regularly issue liturgical directives which are indefensible from either the Anglican tradition or from the tradition of the whole church. When this is brought to their attention they are placed in an embarrassed position which could have been easily avoided had they consulted with a liturgist beforehand. I am unaware of Anglican liturgists whose first commitment is to something other than the life and health of the local church. They are generally more than willing to offer all their experience and training to the resolution of very practical pastoral problems as well as to the more long-term projects of helping to create new liturgical texts for the local church.

It is not the goal of liturgists (as is often unfairly rumoured) to re-create some liturgical golden age, but to help provide the forms that best enable the People of God to worship God and to equip them for their work of proclaiming the gospel and serving Christ in the world. Often their knowledge of the past informs this work, simply because we would be very vain to believe that nothing from our past has anything to say to our present situation, but like other aspects of our Anglican life the tradition lives when it serves the present needs of the church rather than when it acts as a pall suffocating any creative initiative. The second need, then, is to use those with special liturgical formation in the ongoing life of the local church.

(ii) THE LITURGICAL ASSEMBLY

Bishops who have promised to 'encourage and support all the baptized in their gifts and ministries' need to be particularly conscious of how they do this in the context of the many liturgical assemblies in which they find themselves present. These assemblies run from the liturgies of great occasions (like ordinations) to liturgies in small, possibly moribund, parishes. No matter what the occasion there is a particular onus that falls on the bishop as chief pastor and as chief liturgical officer to see that each liturgy is the best possible model of liturgical life.

In liturgies for great occasions this demands that an eye be kept out for particular dangers. Often minor, or functional, parts of the liturgy take on a disproportionate weight. The initial gathering of the community far too easily becomes an overly clericalized spectacle as the laity passively watch hundreds of servers and lay readers as well as all the diocesan clergy process by. On these occasions, too, the diversity of liturgical ministry assured by our new liturgical texts is often seriously violated. There are ordinations to the episcopate in which only bishops exercise liturgical ministries or diocesan ordinations in which there seems to be a need to give all the ordinands a 'job' other than being ordained. The result is often a serious distortion of the liturgy itself: the laity are not allowed to read the first two readings nor a deacon the gospel; responsibility for the prayers of the people becomes clericalized and lay persons who regularly are involved in distributing communion are relegated to the pew. The liturgical model we present on these great occasions should be the church at her best, one that clearly says that 'the celebration of the eucharist is the work of the whole People of God,' not one that clearly says that the liturgy is a clerical activity performed before a passive laity or that the ministry of lay people in the liturgy is only a transient phenomenon which is dispensable when there are sufficient clergy available. So too we should not present models that say that the ministry of priests and deacons is dispensable when there are enough bishops present or that women's ministries are not upheld because some members of the assembly might dispute their legitimacy.

In a derivative sense bishops should also ensure that the liturgical life of their cathedrals and theological colleges offers good liturgical models. The cathedral church of a diocese has a particular responsibility for modelling the best of what the liturgy can be for the local church and usually has both the human and economic resources to do so. Theological colleges have a responsibility for presenting the best liturgical models possible, so that theological students can glimpse a vision of what liturgical life can be, so that they have something to work towards when they find themselves responsible for the liturgical life of a parish.

Visits to parishes also present opportunities for bishops to see that good liturgical modelling is assured. This may be a time when the bishop is called on as teacher, explaining liturgical change in the face of some hostility and ensuring that the rites are observed in the spirit with which they were written. The bishop, as chief liturgical officer, can see that, at least on the occasion of an episcopal visit, the liturgy is celebrated with integrity. (A liturgy well modelled teaches more than many lectures). This may well mean that some balance will have to be achieved in what takes place when the bishop visits i.e. the bishops may come to a parish to teach, preach and preside at the eucharist, rather than allow every visit to be devoted to confirmations or the blessing of the various objects (most of which, should they need any sort of blessing at all, could perfectly well be blessed by the local parish priest) which form the central part of many visitations. Freed from the too-frequent self-definition as 'confirming machine' bishops will be less inclined to devote all their time to young confirmands and spend more time as pastor and teacher with the whole of the local community, addressing themselves to another part of their commission prayed for at the ordination:

'Through him ... unite its members in a holy fellowship of truth and love. Enable him as a true shepherd to feed and govern your flock; make him a wise teacher, and steadfast as guardian of its faith and sacraments. Guide and direct him in presiding at the worship of your people.'

(Church of England, *Alternative Service Book*, p.394)

As a part of presenting a good liturgical model on both great diocesan occasions as well as parochial visits it is imperative that bishops have re-thought their own liturgical style of presiding in the context of the new liturgical texts. It is a betrayal of the integrity of the new texts to impose on them in an uncritical fashion the piety and liturgical gestures associated with the Book of Common Prayer. The Holy Table is not a cloak room on which croziers and mitres are to be rested when not in use. Episcopal prayers at ordinations and confirmations are said standing and without mitre or crozier: it is curious the number of bishops who would never dream of sitting and availing themselves of hat and stick while presiding at the eucharistic prayer who have never extended that conviction to other prayers which are direct parallels to that prayer. Contemporary liturgical preaching is normatively on the lections of the day and not an invariable annual confirmation sermon. An unreflecting use of episcopal ornaments and style of liturgical presidency can seriously undermine all that bishops have built up through their care and nurture of those who are responsible for teaching liturgy in the colleges (and for the liturgical formation of clergy and laity) simply because an increasing number of the faithful will understand the integrity of liturgical sign and gesture and realize that their bishop does not.

CONCLUSION

That has brought us full circle. It should be clear that the place of the bishop in the liturgical life of the diocese and parish is more central and assured in our liturgical texts than it ever has been in our history as Anglicans. The expectations placed on bishops are perhaps also higher than they have ever been. The effect on the morale of a diocese—both of the clergy and laity—when it is apparent that the bishop is fully committed to the renewal of the Christian life in a diocese is transforming. The bishop's commitment to liturgical renewal becomes infectious. This can only have its maximum effect if bishops are prepared to share this ministry: by seeing that those who teach liturgy in the theological colleges have adequate formation in the subject; by seeing that the diocese has a liturgical commission which is concerned for the ongoing liturgical life of the diocese and assists the bishop with liturgical questions and the preparation and celebration of diocesan liturgies; by assuring that liturgical renewal is a part of the continuing education programme of the diocese; and by assuring that all the liturgies at which the bishop presides are the best models possible of the liturgy as the work of the whole People of God. Perhaps at no other time has no much responsibility been given to Anglican bishops for our common liturgical life; the Communion as a whole awaits their positive response.

4. The Bishop in his Cathedral

Opportunities for the liturgical expression of the bishop's ministry in his cathedral depend on a number of complex and inter-related factors, particularly in England, where the day-to-day control of a cathedral and its liturgy is in the hands of the dean (or provost) and chapter. The bishop's task is to serve and build up his diocese, to enable it to be the church. But he will not be able to fulfil this unless he himself is supported. How can a cathedral support its bishop, and help him to give liturgical expression to these thrusts, and how can the bishop help his cathedral to become the bishop's church, a focus for the life and prayer and worship of the whole diocese?

HISTORICAL

To begin to answer this question, we must take a historical glance at the relationship between the bishop and his cathedral. Essentially, a cathedral is the church where the bishop has his 'cathedra', his teaching chair. In the early Christian centuries, the building that contained the bishop's cathedra was not necessarily a church in the terms in which we would understand it now: rather, it was a complex of rooms with at least one large hall, in which the cathedra was set. In these buildings the bishop lived with his household, and the differing rooms began to take on characters according to function: the hall which contained the cathedra came to be set apart for expounding the faith and celecbrating the sacraments, as did the baptistry for rites of initiation. Before there was a settled pattern of Christian communities, regularly meeting independently of the Bishop's community and serviced by one of his presbyters, the cathedral was frequently the only church building in a diocese.

Some of this feel of a community gathered round the bishop was preserved in the years following the Christianization of Britain. Minsters were set up, a group of buildings surrounding a large church which housed a missionary bishop and his staff, and these became the mother church of a number of outlying chapels and estate churches, in and through which the mission of the church could be extended to the surrounding area. The thrust of these churches was primarily outwards, centres where a company of Christians could live in community with their bishop, and to which they could return for rest and renewal. Sometimes the bishop entrusted the life of the minster to a religious community, sometimes to what became a college of secular priests. Either way, as the bishop's jurisdiction grew, he was away more frequently and was less able to be the effecdtive day-to-day head of the cathedral. At the same time, the priests who had been itinerant missionaries now found themselves more or less permanently established as the resident parish priests of small communities, returning to the cathedral and feeling part of that community much less frequently, while the monastic or secular community which ran the cathedral, by now a substantial and powerful head-quarters, began to build up its own rather more inward style of community life, not infrequently on the Benedictine model, with a priority given to liturgical prayer and study. In these divergencies lie the needs of the disjunction in

England between the bishop and his cathedral, leading to the classical situation in the post-Henridian church whereby a dean and chapter run the cathedral, and may or may not invite the bishop to come to it. This disjunction has even been given quasi-liturgical expression in the last hundred years, by having the bishop knock on the cathedral door to demand admission for his enthronement!

The pages of Anthony Trollope's novel are eloquent testimony to the potentially destructive separation of bishop and cathedral. Nor are those days altogether past: but in recent years it has become clear that this disjunction at the heart of a diocese's life is more than potentially destructive: the bishop needs the support of his cathedral and chapter to exercise his ministry, and the cathedral needs the support of its bishop to be the cathedral of the diocese rather than a trap for tourists.

RATIONALES

That cathedrals needed to revise their *raison d'être* was clear to the visionaries of the nineteenth century. It was Dr. Pusey who commended cathedrals to the church as study centres, places of scholarship and training for ministry. During this period a number of theological colleges were founded under the shadow of cathedrals, and until relatively recently it was possible to think of a cathedral canonry as a post for leisured and scholarly reflection. Later in the century, Bishop Benson, of Truro, felt that the justification for a cathedral and its chapter lay in service to the diocese. He believed the canons of the cathedral should act as the Bishop's Council, each being responsible for a separate diocesan activity: training for clergy, the church schools, and evangelism and children's work—a process disparagingly referred to by a recent writer as 'conscripting cathedral chapters into diocesan service'. A further conception, of the cathedral as the mother church of the diocese, open and welcoming to all, is almost entirely due to Dean Bennett of Chester in the 1920s. He saw the cathedral as a venerable church, open and welcoming, in which pilgrims and casual visitors, enquirers after truth and seekers after comfort alike, could find themselves by a building which openly expressed the Christian life and guided them on their way.

In our own time, certain cathedrals have developed distinctive ministries: as the centre of a worldwide ministry of reconciliation, or as a centre of unity in a strife-torn city; some have adopted the style of a parish church writ large, while others can make use of their resources to be a shop-window for the life of the diocese; others again have an overwhelming number of visitors, with the task of turning tourists into pilgrims and pilgrims into worshippers.

What does the vision at the heart of each of these developments have to offer to the bishop's ministry today?

First, a cathedral should give visible expression to the idea of the bishop as a focus of unity in prayer and worship. A cathedral's primary task must be to provide the spiritual focus and heart to the praying life of the diocese. Second, the cathedral is where the bishop has his teaching chair, his cathedra. While many bishops regard teaching the faith as a prime commitment, few of them are able or willing to exercise this ministry unaided: if the cathedra is traditionally the place from which the bishop's teaching ministry is exercised, it is natural for his cathedral building and its staff to be the chief resource in supporting his teaching ministry. Third, the bishop, as the public face of the church, has a prime concern for the church's mission, and unrivalled opportunities to preach to those who come to the cathedral for special services; and the cathedral, too, can help provide opportunities and occasions when leaders in church and community can come together to discuss matters of common concern in public life.

How is this ministry of worship, teaching and mission, a ministry focused in the bishop and shared with his cathedral, to be given liturgical expression?

ORDINATION

First, just as all ministry in the diocese coheres and finds its expression in the bishop, so it is important for the rites of ordination and confirmation, two distinctive, though parallel, episcopal rites, to be focused in his cathedral.

It is by the sacrament of orders that the church's ministry is shaped and formed, and given visible expression. Each order expresses a distinctive aspect of the church's ministry. But ordination is neither for the person, nor for the local church alone. To ordain candidates in local churches where their vocation has been nurtured or in which they are, or will be, serving, is to run the risk of losing sight of the essential catholicity of orders, of the fact that it is the relationship of the ordained ministers to each other and to their bishop which gives shape and form in a church which so often seems local and parochial. A misleading impression can easily be created if a diocesan bishop goes to a parish church where a deacon is already serving in order to ordain him to the priesthood. This confusion is made worse if the ordaining minister is not the diocesan or area bishop, but some assistant or retired minister in episcopal orders who has no necessarily continuing relationship with the candidate he has just ordained. If an ordination of a single priest or deacon cannot take place in the cathedral building, then might not members of the chapter go with the bishop so that it is clear that the cathedral is, in this sense, mobile, and has come to the parish?

As a norm, ordinations should take place in the cathedral. Here, visible expression can be given to the sense of diocesan family, and to the idea that the conferring of orders is an act of the universal church. Although it is the custom in some places to ordain deacons and priests at the same service, such combined ordinations seem to emphasize a hierarchical approach to orders, that the diaconate is a stepping-stone to the priesthood. Growing awareness of the distinctive vocation of diaconal ministry in its own right, as something basic to all ministries and yet complementary to that of the priesthood and episcopate, has led a growing number of bishops to ordain to the diaconate and priesthood at separate services. At the moment in the Church of England there are likely to be a variety of candidates for ordination to the diaconate, the transitional male deacons expecting to proceed to the priesthood, and women deacons, together with a growing number of male deacons, who believe that their vocation is to the distinctive diaconate. Such ordinations to the diaconate will draw together a very diverse group of people, and their ordination in the cathedral is a powerful reminder to the diocese as a whole—and indeed to the cathedral—that the foundation of a rich diversity of ministry in Christ is service.

There are ways in which this might be given fuller expression than is provided for in most Ordinals. Although the ASB Ordinal says 'It is appropriate that the newly-ordained should be invited by the Bishop to exercise their new ministry in the course of the service,' it is not always apparent what this means. The simplest way in which it can be given expression is by the newly-ordained deacons being invited to prepare the gifts at the Holy Table, and to assist in the distribution of communion. How far this scripturally-based (Acts 6.2ff.) liturgical tradition makes the point of the diaconate is open to question: a more vivid—and equally scriptural—sign is for the bishop, having ordained the candidates deacon and given the New Testament to each one, to wash their feet. This is a memorable and effective sign for those who are today enrolled into Christ's ministry of service to have their bishop put aside his garments, and having girded himself with a towel, pour water into a basin and begin to wash the feet of his new deacons.

Ordinations to the priesthood are accompanied by their own signs, the singing of the Veni Creator and the Giving of the Bible: again, while it may be desirable for the ordaining bishop to give a copy of the Bible to each of those he is ordaining to mark the occasion, that is not the liturgical point which is being made: it is 'The Bible' not a copy of the Bible, which is being given to each of the newly-ordained priests in turn, and only if each candidate receives into his hands in turn a copy of the cathedral's largest Bible, is the point made that to each is being entrusted the preaching and teaching of the faith which we hold in common: the diversity of individual ministers and ministries is held together by the expression of allegiance to the same visible text, as the dispensed authority to celebrate the sacraments and to preach and is held together by allegiance to, and commission from, the one bishop.

BAPTISM AND CONFIRMATION

But it is not only at ordinations the bishop's ministry as the focus of unity in the diocese is made visible. At baptism and confirmation, especially when adults are present, the same is true. While confirmation completes the process of initiation begun in baptism, it has, within the Anglican tradition, where confirmation is reserved to the bishop, meant other things as well. It is the sacrament which introduces the Christian to the diocese as the basic unit of the church, and to the bishop as the chief pastor of it, and to full communion with the bishop.

This is not always evident. If a bishop confirms largely at parish confirmations, although the bishop (? a bishop) comes, he comes to the parish, and it becomes a parochial event, rather than a diocesan event. And the more a bishop comes to parishes primarily to confirm, the less time he has for visiting parishes apart from confirmations, and therefore the less opportunity he has of meeting the normal worshipping congregation. And, because of the understandable impossibility of the bishop visiting all parishes for confirmations as often as they would like, the use of assistant bishops and suffragans has become necessary, with all the resulting pastoral and theological confusion as to who 'the' bishop is.

Of course there will always be a mixed economy in the Anglican dispensation, and it would be churlish of a bishop who had gone to celebrate the parish eucharist to refuse to baptize or confirm candidates presented to him. But the opportunity of a number of services of baptism and confirmation at the cathedral is one that the bishop should consider seriously. The cathedral has the resources to make such a service—and all such services should and could have echoes of the powerful and dramatic Easter Vigil—a truly memorable and inspiring event, and likewise the resources to offer the opportunity for the bishop to meet and talk to large numbers of people who are perhaps only loosely attached to the life of the church. There are great evangelistic opportunities in such a celebration, and it can give a sense of unity and impetus to the whole life of the diocese. Such a service held at six o'clock on a Saturday evening, or on the vigils of great festivals, can readily stand on its own without the addition of a communion service, and, by using the whole space of the cathedral, can allow candidates a sense of turning from darkness to light, a sense of movement and journey through the cathedral, as they declare the faith of their baptism, and come to the bishop for confirmation.

There are additional pastoral reasons for suggesting such a programme. The changing patterns of parish life today mean that a regular annual fixture is not always easy. Many parishes welcome the chance of bringing a few candidates to a series of confirmations throughout the year: patterns of faith-sharing and nurture promoted by the catechumenate network and the Roman Catholic 'Rite of Christian Initiation of Adults' take the development of adult Christian discipleship more seriously, with a 'right time' on the journey to celebrate the sacraments which a yearly fixed date cannot accommodate. Moreover, the candidates need to learn, and to experience, that they are not merely members of the parish of St. Mildred's, but members of the whole church of God, with gifts to share and contribute, but much to learn from others as well, as members of the wider diocesan family

In the Anglican tradition the bishop has always been the minister of confirmation, and in the context of the growing number of adult confirmations of those who have not previously been baptized, it is worth remembering that Canon B24—'Of the Baptism of such as are of riper years'—makes notification of adult baptism to the bishop mandatory.[1] That baptism and confirmation of adults are two parts of the same rite does not need to be argued these days. But there are still some ministers who prefer to baptize their adults privately beforehand, either because they feel that the candidates might be embarrassed at not already being baptized—though the number of adults who have not been baptized before they come to confirmation these days is growing—or because they feel that baptism is something that they would prefer to do themselves. In this context it is worth pointing out that although the bishop presides over the whole rite of initiation, over the ministry of the word, the baptism and the confirmation, it is perfectly proper for him to delegate certain parts and functions to other ministers, and cerainly, when it comes to baptizing, he does not have to baptize

---

[1] This is a modern Canon of the Church of England (as is the one quoted in footnote opposite), and may not recur in quite this way in other Provinces. It reflects the 1662 rubric that *timely notice* be given to the bishop—probably so that he could monitor the return of Anabaptists to the fold!—Editor.

each individual himself any more than he has to administer communion to each individual—a very clear index of how serious he is about sharing his ministry.

At any such confirmation in the cathedral, as well as at ordinations, the bishop will be supported by his chapter, together with other priests associated with the candidates, whose task is to support the bishop in his prayers for the candidates, and to make visible the fact that the bishop does not act alone.

BLESSING OF OILS

This sense of solidarity with the bishop is given formal expression in another distinctively cathedral occasion, when the bishop meets with his clergy, traditionally on Maundy Thursday morning, to bless the oils.[1] There is oil for anointing the sick; for the signing with the cross after the Decision at baptism (ASB, p.225 note 3); and for confirmation by the bishop (p.226 note 7).[2] The oils are distributed to the priests after being blessed by the bishop, and are a visible link between the bishop and the ministry of healing. The presence of all the clergy with their bishop to receive the newly-blessed oils has led to this being an occasion when they together affirm their participation in the ministry of Christ thereby entrusted to them, and renew the promises made at their ordination. This is an occasion of great value in the life of the diocese, when the bond between the bishop and his clergy can be deepened.

LITURGICAL PRESIDENCY

On such occasions, when the bishop comes and celebrates the eucharist with the cathedral chapter, the question of how the clergy assisting can express that unity arises. For some, the automatic answer will be that the clergy should 'concelebrate' with the bishop. Others, while wishing to find a way of expressing their assistance in the celebration, are not happy with any pattern which might imply the necessity or even desirability of 'co-consecration'.

Within such a celebration, of which the ordained minister is the focus, the presidency cannot be shared, only supported. Such support seems to be natural and appropriate, particularly when the bishop presides in such a place as a cathedral, where the life of prayer and worship is shared and supported by a 'college' of priests. Such support is often best expressed by the unanimity of simple gestures which indicate solidarity with the presiding minister, such as uplifted arms throughout the eucharistic prayer, rather than by an attempt to speak the prayers together in a motley unison. In addition, there must be adequate space around the holy table, and in practice this means a free-standing table in an empty sanctuary or at the head of the nave. A celebration whch is crowded or cluttered, and which exhibits a lack of verbal unanimity or confused or variant gesture or vesture is likely to be a source of irritation or confusion to the congregation.

---

[1] Canon B37 states that '. . . pure olive oil consecrated by the bishop of the diocese, or else by the priest himself . . . ' is what should be used for the anointing of the sick. See Ministry to the Sick (1983).

[2] No authorized text for the actual consecration of these three oils has yet been approved by the General Synod of the Church of England.

In this I am assuming that the bishop, when he comes to the cathedral, will be the presiding minister at any eucharistic rite. While that will be the norm, there may be occasions when the bishop wishes to delegate presiding at the celebration to someone else: for example, when a priest in the diocese celebrates an anniversary, or on family occasions like a funeral or marriage, or when—as can frequently occur on major feasts—two principal eucharists follow each other in quick succession and the bishop presides at one and preaches at the other. On such occasions, the bishop's presidency should be acknowledged by no more than a bow at the beginning and by his giving the blessing at the end of the rite.

And the cathedral itself, that permanent symbol of the bishop's responsibility to speak to and for the church: where should it be placed, and how should it be used? The Archbishop of Canterbury speaking in his cathedral on Christmas morning speaks more powerfully and perhaps shows more clearly what an episcopal statement is than if he makes it in a television studio or writes a letter to *The Times* from his study at Lambeth. Speaking in his cathedral, the bishop can be seen to be articulating the apostolic gospel from within the context of the developing tradition, rather than speaking his mind as an individual. Should bishops be encouraged to aim, when making public statements, to do so as often as they can in their cathedrals?

CATHEDRAL, BISHOP, AND DIOCESE

What this essay is doing is sketching a style of worship for gatherings that are truly diocesan in significance, which neither the bishop nor the cathedral acting in isolation would necessarily arrive at. Left to its own devices, a cathedral can often drift into its own world, a world formed by the English choral tradition, and the very Anglican and incarnational thrust of the regular recitation of the divine office on the one hand, and the specific celebrations of carol services and Judges' services, of services for industry and for the Children's Society set within the rhythm of the regular offering of the eucharist on the other. This conjunction between the regular and the occasional, between the traditional and the immediate, between that at which we are wondering spectators and that in which we are active participants, is distinctively different in almost every aspect from the regular worship of parish churches up and down the diocese. In a sense the two do not meet, and we should not be surprised at this. Neither the cathedral nor the parochial tradition, on its own, provide a suitable vehicle for those acts of worship led by the bishop in his cathedral which we have been describing. It is no good treating the cathedral as if it were a parish church writ large: the spaces, the scale and the resources are different. Nor is it more plausible to graft such events on to the marvellous, but relatively static and non-participatory Anglican cathedral tradition. Each cathedral needs to evolve a style of worship for such occasions which is genuinely 'diocesan' rather than 'cathedral', and in which parish congregations can come and feel at home, but yet one which resonates with a depth of understanding no individual parish could produce on its own.

In or from the cathedral, the bishop and his chapter, by focusing on a number of specific rites in which they are necessarily both involved—the eucharist of chrism, the Easter Vigil, services of baptism and confirmation, the ordinations—have the chance of creating a sense of style in worship which the bishop can carry with him where he goes, and which will help create a sense of diocesan unity. I do not mean that the bishop should slavishly adopt one style: like any other president, he needs to be sensitive to the needs of the people among whom he is ministering, and to learn to work 'with the grain'. But if the bishop's ministry is formed and undergirded by a sense of liturgical belonging, if the bishop feels himself to be part of his cathedral and not always a footloose nomad, then he may find it easier to participate in the acts of worship he meets in the different parishes of the diocese, without feeling the constant need to assert his own liturgical style as an individual. Conversely, if the members of the chapter and cathedral staff have opportunities to share in parochial worship, then they too will find opportunity to draw back into the worshipping life of the cathedral what they have learned from their visits to parishes. In this way, bridges can be built and the riches of different styles and traditions shared in a way that is inclusive, not in the sense of seeking uniformity in the lowest common denominator, but in the sense of valuing that unity which comes from an appreciation of the rich diversity of styles and traditions.

In each of the specific 'cathedral liturgies' mentioned above, there is a sense of movement, of redemptive change, of growth in and through the liturgical action. While this is something that should be true of any good liturgical act—that starting at one place you are transported to another—it is particularly true of those specific cathedral liturgies: the bishop is not only the focus of unity around whom the people of God in the diocese may gather; he is also the pastor of his people, leading them on through the rugged wilderness to the promised land. Whether the cathedral is an old pilgrimage church or not, its size and scale, and not infrequently its division into two or more spaces, makes it particularly suitable for such celebrations. At the cathedral, a diverse congregation may be led through an act of worship to something new which lies beyond what they had ever imagined. This is something which it is not easy to experience in your own church: familiar patterns in the relatively confined space of a well-known building conspire against this. But to leave your own parish church, to go at the bishop's invitation to his cathedral, and to join with fellow-worshippers from other parishes, is to allow the possibility not only of recognizing your membership within the worshipping life of the whole diocesan family, but also of having your vision enlarged beyond the bounds you had imagined possible.

To achieve this requires a degree of trust and a sense of commitment on the part of the bishop to the cathedral and its distinctive ministry, and on the part of the cathedral to the bishop in the support of his ministry. Without the bishop, the cathedral can easily become a prisoner of its own beautiful world. Without the cathedral, the bishop can easily become submerged in a scrapbook succession of parochial experiences which succeed each other week by week. Bishop and cathedral need each other, and need to learn to respect each other for the enrichment of the worship, nurture and mission of the church.

The Bishop in his Cathedral 39

5. The Bishop Sets Out

'A bishop of the Church of England has to have many of the qualities of an old theatrical trouper. He sets out on a circuit with a hazy, unreliable memory of the peculiarities of the next "house" in which he is to perform and wondering which version of the script they are expecting him to use. Yet, besides studying the whims of each audience and being "all things to all men", he has to believe in what he is doing and satisfy himself that each detail serves the total effect that he wants to communicate.'[1]

So Bishop John Taylor has written, and many a bishop will recognize himself in that, whether he be of the Church of England or of another Anglican province. Every church is expecting something different, and indeed every church has the right to expect something different, for to some extent the bishop has to be sensitive to local style and ethos. But there are limits on that, for the bishop, like the local congregation, must have his integrity. He must be himself, and be sufficiently relaxed in the liturgy to communicate that authenticity without which his leadership of worship will be sadly impoverished. The bishop must have his 'style', and, more than that, he must have some ground rules so that he does not have to think anew in every fresh situation, lest he be diverted by detail from the overall spirit of the liturgy. To some extent he can learn some rules from a book like this, but it is doubtful whether he can, or should, be spared the trouble of having to decide at least some principles for himself. Authenticity, which does not have to be eccentricity, needs to be worked at.

He sets out on a typical Sunday; if he is one of the privileged few, with his chauffeur, and the chaplain who has packed the bags.[2] More likely he is himself the packer and the driver. What must he pack and put into the car?

STAFF

The pastoral staff, whether genuine shepherd's crook, as is the fashion at least in countries where genuine shepherds have crooks, or more stylized crozier, will nearly always have its place in the boot. When he gets to his destination, how is the bishop to use it? It is essentially a walking stick. Time was when bishops followed a strange fashion of having their pastoral staffs carried in front of them in the style of a processional cross. It may have added to their grandeur, but it certainly did nothing to convey the picture of the shepherd—more like the golfer with his caddy carrying the clubs! There are pockets of the church where this custom still survives, but it does need some gentle questioning.

---

[1] John V. Taylor in the foreword to Michael Perjam *Liturgy Pastoral and Parochial* (SPCK, 1984).

[2] Perhaps it is only in England that these privileged few exist. If, at points, this essay is very English, the author apologizes, excuses himself on the grounds that these principles must be earthed in the reality of one province, and asks the reader to translate into terms that make sense in different cultural and social settings.

At least on entering and leaving the church in procession the bishop uses his staff. Clearly it would be over-fussy for him to take it with him on every little walk-about during the liturgy. For most of the time it can stand by his chair. Just occasionally it seems best to place it on the holy table, but on the whole it is better, especially at the eucharist, if the table can be free of episcopal impedimenta so that bread and wine can stand out uncluttered as the focus of the celebration.

As to when the bishop needs the staff during the liturgy, it is almost universal custom that he takes it into his left hand to give the blessing. In Anglicanism, it has also become usual for staff (and mitre) to highlight the absolution. This is less obviously right. If the absolution is regarded as a prayer, and it is more clearly so when the 'us' rather than the 'you' form is employed, then the staff, and certainly the mitre (but see below), seem superfluous. In the modern Roman ceremonial, the bishop takes the staff into his hand while the Gospel is read. Such a gesture gives emphasis to the bishop's role as teacher and guardian of the faith. It is a helpful piece of symbolism. It also seems appropriate for the bishop to hold his staff as he lays his hand on the head of confirmands.[1] This makes more sense when he is standing to do so. When the words he employs are a prayer to God, standing is certainly the better posture.

The bishop may think he should not bother to take his staff if he is going outside his diocese. Here recent Anglican practice seems to be at odds with a longer, and probably more theological, position. Anglican bishops have on the whole regarded the staff as a sign of *jurisdiction*, and have therefore carried it only within their own dioceses. But the staff is given at the ordination of a bishop[2] as sign of his episcopal *office*, rather than of particular jurisdiction, and it might be better if it were generally agreed that a bishop presiding at the liturgy might use a staff, irrespective of where he was.[3] Some Anglican bishops and diocese follow this broader view already, but they are probably not yet the majority. Though a contrary case could be made, it does seem best that only the bishop who presides should carry a staff.

A word may be said here about the archiepiscopal cross. Here, again, there has developed an Anglican practice at odds with the western tradition, though quite in line with Orthodox custom. Unlike the staff, the archiepiscopal cross *is* a processional cross, and should therefore be carried in front of the archbishop. But should he use it as staff when blessing? If an archbishop used his crozier whenever he was, even outside his diocese, there might not be the temptation to seize

---

[1] The rubrics in most of our provinces are clear that the bishop confirms with *one* hand on the candidate's head (unlike ordination where it is 'hands').

[2] Anglican ordinals vary. For instance in the English ASB 1980 the staff *may* be given. In the Canadian BAS it *is* given.

[3] This is possibly an over-simplification, though a helpful one. It could be said that the staff is a sign of jurisdiction, but of episcopal jurisdiction inherent in the office, not of particular geographical jurisdiction. Given that every bishop receives both the office and a particular jurisdiction, the problem, if there is one, comes not at consecration but after resignation.

the cross and bless with it. But, when all is said and done, the use of the archiepiscopal cross in blessing does not give any wrong signals, and is probably best regarded as an established and harmless Anglican custom that does not warrant challenge.[1]

ROBES

Packing the staff for the journey is an easy matter compared with selecting the right robes or vestments for the suitcase. Anglican episcopal vesture has become unnecessarily complicated, and there is need for bold simplification.[2]

The first choice before the bishop is whether choir dreess is to be worn or cope (or chasuble at the eucharist) and mitre. In some provinces, most parishes have expected the bishop to preside at the sacraments in cope and mitre. They may well also have expected a cope and mitre for other rather grand occasions of a non-sacramental nature. But, where the other clergy are to wear choir dress of surplice, scarf and hood, the bishop is perfectly right to wear the episcopal equivalent. This is rochet, chimere and scarf. Purple or black caps, carried but not worn, seem an unnecessary addition, and other simplifications could be considered, including the abandonment of the hood which had no historical place with the chimere. The rochet, which is simply a development of the alb, might well return to that form and lose the fussy wristbands and cuffs. The complication with the chimere is that it is now customary for all bishops, even those who are not doctors, to wear a red one on the majority of occasions, and the black more rarely.[3] An agreement by all bishops to use one colour or the other would make for a welcome simplification.

But it is the cope and mitre that has emerged as the most common form of episcopal dress in many provinces. This is strange when the cope has no partiuclar episcopal connotations historically! The cope has never been subject to quite such a rigid rule about liturgical colour as, say, the stole or chasuble. Bishops often have a design or combination of colours that will do for almost all seasons. Where a particular colour is being used, it is important to note that there has been a move away from the use of gold/white for almost every sacramental form to the use of the red of the Holy Spirit at ordinations, and sometimes at confirmations, though when confirmation forms part of a full initiation liturgy that includes baptism, the gold/white is probably to be preferred.

There is a custom, still alive in some parts of the church, of taking off the cope to preach. Unless the pulpit is very small and the bishop in cope fairly large, this

---

[1] At this and other points this book disagrees with *Episcopal Services* which relied heavily on Roman practice, and, even within its own terms, is now out of date.

[2] This essay proceeds on the assumption that the bishop has this huge, expensive and complicated episcopal wardrobe. But should he have it? Should not the Lambeth bishops look seriously at a simplification of their dress, which looks quaint and fussy in an English situation (in the televised House of Lords, for instance), and more so in other countries where climate and local traditions suggest something very different?

[3] This is because in England it has been the correct outfit for Convocation.

is an over-fussy bit of ceremonial, and in these days when copes are not often of such heavy fabric as in the past, quite unnecessary. The sermon is as much part of both the liturgy and the bishop's ministry as anything else (more so than some things), and to take off the cope to preach says the wrong things about the bishop and preaching. But, if the cope has to be removed, at least let it not be draped across the altar like a cultic shroud. The bishop should leave his clothes on the holy table no more than anybody else.

In some churches it is a chasuble that the bishop wears when celebrating the eucharist. What the bishop wears at the eucharist should not be dictated by his own preference. In many provinces, as in England, vesture for the eucharist in a particular church is decided by long custom or by a decision of the Church Council. The bishop has no more right than any other celebrant to dispense with local practice in this matter.[1] A bishop is not usually expected to bring his own chasuble, but to use that which the church provides. Indeed there is a certain theological point in seeing him dressed in what the parish priest normally wears each Sunday, rather than is some rather grander outfit. What is undesirable and without meaning is changing garments half-way through; confirming, for instance, in cope, and then presiding at the eucharist in chasuble. Whatever is to be worn should be worn throughout.

MITRE

The mitre is probably the most distinctive piece of episcopal regalia, and also symbolically the most esoteric, though John Halliburton has done his best to give it meaning.[2] In some provinces where it was not previously worn, it has suddenly blossomed into use, often rather eccentrically. There is no precedent for the use of the mitre except with cope or chasuble. With choir dress it is found only on eighteenth century tombs!

The current Roman provisions recognize only two sorts of mitre—gold and white, gold ordinarily, but white for funerals, some other less festal occasions, and for any bishop other than the president when many gathered together. Among Anglicans a custom has developed of having the mitre designed to 'match' the cope in terms of colour and decoration. There is nothing wrong with this, except possibly cost; it probably necessitates several different mitres. The traditional plain gold or plain white does allow it to be worn with any liturgical colour or design.

Each bishop needs his own rationale for when he wears and does not wear his mitre during the liturgy. In the past there was often a very fussy taking on and off at frequent points during the liturgy. One way of approaching the matter is to wear it during the procession in, take it off on arrival at the chair or holy table,

---

[1] In England a custom grew up that some bishops would decline to wear a chasuble, and would wear a cope in defiance of local practice. This belonged to the days when the legality of eucharistic vestments was a matter of dispute. Now that they are, without doubt, proper and legal vesture, a bishop has no right to ride roughshod over the local practice. Equally the canons assure him that in wearing them he is not adopting a particular doctrinal stance about the eucharist.

[2] See above, p.18.

and not put it on again until the blessing. Another approach is, additionally, to wear it when sitting down. But there is no precedent for wearing it for the Gospel—the bishop stands bare-headed because he is under obedience to the Gospel—though there is for preaching. Rather too many bishops wear it to pray. There is a tendency to put it on before solemn liturgical moments, such as confirming or ordaining, but these are essentially moments of prayer, more clearly so in the new liturgies than in the older ones based on the Prayer Book. In general the old tradition of the seated mitred bishop confirming or ordaining needs to give way to the standing bare-headed bishop praying as he confirms or ordains.[1] In general, if a bishop is worried by takings on and off, he is better with the mitre off through most of the liturgy than with it on. This has never been better expressed than by Bishop Frere: 'Don't pray in it and don't fuss with it!'

As with the staff, there is the question of where it should be when not on the bishop's head! Under his arm, or clutched with a hymn book in his hand, seems undignified. Better that it be put down. If this has to be on the altar, let it be flat, drawing as little attention to itself as possible. Another quite eccentric custom has been that of the mitre stood on the altar like an episcopal tea-cosy. The holy table is for the eucharist, and it is bread and a cup of wine that should be the focus on it; it is not a display chest for episcopal insignia.

LITURGICAL PRESIDENCY

So with the suitcase safely in the car, the bishop is off, with a ring on his finger and a cross on his chest (and it should be on his chest rather than dangling at his middle), driving to the parish, trying to reconcile his spirituality and theirs so that both may be enriched. He arrives. What of the liturgy that is now to begin?

The bishop needs to be clear that he is the president of the liturgy. That does not mean that he must do everything himself, but that he should retain to himself certain elements in the service that are moments that focus unity. The various modern Anglican service books have some variety in their approach to presidency, but they are united in expecting the bishop, like any eucharistic president, to retain to himself the opening greeting, the collect, the absolution, the peace, the taking, giving thanks and breaking, and the blessing. This is not because these are all exclusive functions of either the episcopate or the presbyterate, but because they are the points in the service that draw the assembly together. With strong leadership at these points, delegation at other points does not destroy the unity and coherence of the liturgy.

The theological reasons why the bishop should be the eucharistic president when he comes to a church have been already shown.[2] In the past, presidency has often been understood as little more than sitting in the chair and, as far as the eucharist was concerned, absolving, preaching and blessing, while the parish priest was the 'celebrant'. In terms of our renewed understanding of ministry,

---

[1] The contrary argument is that in a Church which does not signal authority very clearly to its people, the seated mitred bishop has been one of the few pictures of authority that ordinary Anglicans have recognized. Some see in its gradual disappearance a real loss.

[2] See above, chapters 1 and 2.

this will not do. To preside is above all to say the eucharistic prayer.[1] This cannot usually be delegated without doing theological injury to the service. Nor does it make sense for parts of the prayer to be delegated, as if they were of less significance than others. In particular the delegation of the opening dialogue to a cantor is to miss entirely the function of that opening exchange whereby the people give the president authority and encouragement to proceed.[2] If the bishop cannot sing the music to which the parish is accustomed, then on that occasion the words should be said, rather than sung.

That said, it is right and proper that all sorts of other parts of the eucharistic liturgy should be delegated. The bishop need not, normally should not, read the scripture readings or the prayers of intercession. He certainly need not invite the people to confess their sins, nor make the various announcements that help the rite along, nor prepare the holy table for the celebration. If the service is to have a satisfactory balance between the ministries of presbyter, deacon and people, these are all parts of it that he should delegate. He may also delegate the distribution of the bread and wine.

INITIATION

Within the celebration of Christian initiation there is also room for delegation. This is particularly important in relation to baptism before confirmation. Modern Anglican initiation rites are united in assuming that, where candidates for confirmation need first to be baptized, this is to happen within the confirmation liturgy, rather than on some, probably more private, occasion in advance of it.[3] The once widespread habit of baptizing before the day of the confirmation, has been strongly discouraged in the recent rites, but has survived by a collusion by bishop and parish priest. The motive of the bishop is not often clear; in the case of the parish priest it is usually a mixture of a desire to save the candidate embarrassment and a desire by the parish priest himself to baptize a candidate in whose preparation for initiation he has had a large part. But embarrassment, never a very justifiable excuse, scarcely applies now that public and adult baptism is so common, and the parish priest's desire to be involved can simply be met through the exercise of delegation in the baptism itself. The bishop ought himself to question the candidates and to say the prayer over the water. He may certainly delegate the ceremonies of the sign of the cross and the giving of the light, and the tradition gives every justification also for delegating the washing in the name of the Trinity.[4] The whole rite, with baptism, confirmation and admission to the eucharist can be celebrated together, with the bishop as its president, but with a proper and significant role for those ministers who have been

---

[1] It is unfortunate that ASB 1980 allows the bishop, unlike any other eucharistic president, to delegate the saying of the eucharistic prayer. This is only defensible in rare circumstances, such as when an archbishop visits another province, or a priest is celebrating a personal jubilee in the presence of his bishop.

[2] As recently as 1987 precisely this happened in York Minster during the General Synod eucharist when a cantor took over from the archbishop the opening dialogue.

[3] This is not the place to discuss the unresolved question of what theological meaning is given to a confirmation that follows immediately after an adult baptism.

[4] This provision for delegation is not necessarily paralleled in other Anglican rites—Editor.

involved in the preparation of the candidates. There is a need for some bishops to make it clearer to their clergy that baptism is an integral part of the initiation rite over which the bishop presides.[1]

The most sensitive area of the service where the bishop may be asked to share the leadership is in the eucharistic action itself. The last fifteen years have seen the development of a number of practices loosely described as 'concelebration'. How is the bishop to respond to the question in the vestry before the service: 'Do you mind if we concelebrate with you?' Indeed, is he to go further, and ask that this happen, and, if so, what exactly is he asking for theologically and liturgically?

There is some variety in the way that modern Anglican prayer books treat the issue. In Canada, for instance, a rubric states that 'it is appropriate that other priests who may be present stand with the celebrant at the altar during the eucharistic prayer, and join in the breaking of bread and in the ministration of communion', and in the American 1979 rite concelebration is advocated at ordinations, whereas in England, concelebration receives only the mildest of hints in the rubrics of the ASB ordinal:'It is appropriate that the newly ordained should be invited by the bishop to exercise their new ministry in the course of the service.' It is not possible, within the confines of this short book, to examine the whole theology of concelebration, and this has been done more adequately for the Church of England by its own Liturgical Commission[2] and by Dr. John Fenwick.[3] Sufficient to say here that there seems to be a kind of Anglican consensus that sees, at the least, no harm and, at best, positive gain in the grouping of priests around the president and their involvement with the eucharisitic action through gesture, but which strongly discourages their joining in the president's words, whether together in a sort of choral speaking or, worse, by dividing the paragraphs of the eucharistic prayer between them.

This latter form, verbal concelebration or 'co-consecration', is the form prescribed in the Roman instructions, which are now themselves twenty-five years old and, as many Roman liturgists feel, ripe for revision. It reflects there a different sort of emphasis on the role of distinctive ministries in the total eucharistic celebration, a different pastoral need in providing the means for a minister to express his priesthood liturgically (Anglican priests have not, with few exceptions, grown up in a world that expects every priest to celebrate daily, but Romans had, (before the Council), and have a theology of the eucharistic prayer that is closer to 'consecration by formula' than most Anglican theologians would want to justify. All these differences make 'verbal concelebration' in an Anglican setting inappropriate. In addition, it is undeniable that choral speaking is an unsatisfactory way of proclaiming powerful words that call for the strong clear voice of a president. Bishops may confidently decline to stage a verbal concelebration.

---

[1] In England there has been a quite frequent tampering with the order of the full initiation rite by bishops who find the movement to the font awkward at the point it is given, but such tampering impoverishes the rite liturgically and should be resisted.

[2] *Concelebration in the Eucharist* (Church House Bookshop, 1982).

[3] *Eucharistic Concelebration* (Grove Worship Series no. 82, 1982).

'Silent' or 'ceremonial' concelebration provides no such problems. It often seems as appropriate today for a bishop to preside at the eucharist with his presbyters groups around him as in the days of Hippolytus.[1] If the geography of the sanctuary allows it, the bishop may welcome this sort of concelebration, and there are particular episcopal occasions when it makes a special point. At a diocesan celebration the bishop may want his area, suffragan or assistant bishops to concelebrate with him. In a cathedral he may want the priests of the cathedral chapter to concelebrate with him. At an ordination he may want the newly ordained priests to concelebrate with him. But in all these cases concelebration means simply that they are grouped around the president, that they employ appropriate gestures that accord with the president's own, and that they assist with the breaking of the bread, where this is a real task rather than a momentary symbol. Concelebration of this sort does not call, logically, for each priest to communicate himself as in the Roman rite.

But there are two important warnings, even with this simple and silent form of concelebration. The first is against its use in the kind of setting where the majority of the 'congregation' will end up grouped around the bishop.[2] For instance, if the eucharist for the blessing of oils on Maundy Thursday is an occasion when the majority of people present are priests, it cannot be a proper setting for concelebration by them all, without creating an extraordinary imbalance in the liturgy. But, secondly, the solution is never concelebration by just *some* of the presbyters, while others sit in the chancel and yet others in the 'congregation'. If the grouping of the clergy around their bishop is saying something theological, it must be a case of all or none—in a cathedral all its chapter or none, in a team ministry all its members or none, on a deanery occasion all the deanery chapter or none, else it says all the *wrong* things about the bishop's relationship with his clergy. Concelebration must never to a matter of choosing six or eight clergy to make it all look nice; aesthetically-determined concelebration is to be avoided.

In this discussion the word 'concelebration' has been used for convenience and simplicity's sake, but, on the whole, except for a sort of liturgical shorthand in planning worship, it is very doubtful whether the word needs to be used. Certainly every eucharist is a concelebration in the sense that the president celebrates with the people of God. And all that is happening in the kind of service described above is that, in that concelebration by the people of God, the presbyters present stand and do things that relate their ministry to that of the president and affirm their relationship with him. To call that aspect of the total action 'concelebration' seems to put all the emphasis on what is, in the end, just a useful point of detail.

GETTING IN PLACE

As he surveys the church from the vestry before the service, the bishop will inevitably wonder where and on what he is to sit. Experience has taught him that,

---

[1] G. J. Cuming (ed.) *Hippolytus: a Text for Students* (Grove Liturgical Study no. 8, 1976).
[2] This is delightfully and memorably conveyed by Peter Ashton in his cover picture to John Fenwick's *Eucharistic Concelebration.*

in some parishes, his visit is the only opportunity to put into use some very grand, high-backed and dreadfully uncomfortable chair. He may want to question gently the use of this, and not only because of comfort. The bishop does indeed need a chair. If it is raised up, it is only so that his presidency may be visible, not because he needs to be raised up to enhance his dignity. In these days when the use of a chair by the eucharistic president is so much more common, it is appropriate that it be *that* chair in which the bishop sits, for this says something about the relationship between the bishop's and the parish priest's presidency of the eucharist. The bishop will not normally need the chair at the moment when he confirms, ordains, or blesses as he licenses.[1] The chair does not therefore always need to be placed in some focal place such as at the chancel step. Presidency is normally a more subtle thing than that. In any case care should be taken not to arrange the furniture in general, and the chair in particular, as to seem to exclude the holy table from the action of the liturgy or to give the chair undue prominence.

All is now ready. The bishop, vested for the occasion, with staff in his left hand, is set to enter the church, perhaps, especially if it is his first visit, to be greeted at the door by the people.[2] Will he carry in his right hand the diocesan form of printed service, whether for confirmation, or ordination, or celebration of a new ministry? He will be tempted to have authorized such a publication, and he will probably have a liturgical committee just waiting to devise it. But he should pause for thought. From his own personal point of view it certainly makes things easier. He knows, wherever he goes, approximately what he will have to say or do. Without it, in many parishes he will find himself in the midst of badly ordered imbalanced liturgy with texts and rubrics inadequately set out on scruffy duplicated sheets. But still he should pause for thought. One of the great joys for the church in our own day has been the loosening up of rubrics to allow for the service to be tailor-made to the occasion and to the community where it is being celebrated. Strong rules on shape and basic texts for important unifying parts of the service leave room for local initiative and sensitive enrichment. The bishop, of all people, should be showing how this can be done, not reducing it all to a predictable uniformity. Whether for the sake of the church, or for his own spiritual growth, he needs to be on the look-out for the staleness that the 'one route only' diocesan form may bring. The age of the word processor makes it easier for there to be a decent tailor-made order for every occasion without undue labour.

So, at the rear of the procession, the bishop steps out into the liturgy. He has worked away in advance at the ground rules of his role in worship, and found the style that is the right meeting point between the tradition and his own liturgical comfort, in order that the celebration over which he presides may have integrity and authenticity. He has done so also in order to be so absorbed in it and taken over by it, that, like every good leader of worship, he may be set free from irksome detail to *pray* the liturgy and thus to help the people to do so too.

---

[1] See above, p.44.
[2] For a text of such a welcome, see Michael Perham *Liturgy Pastoral and Parochial* (SPCK, 1984), p.223.

6. The Bishop in Action

Our theme in this Symposium is the role of the bishop in the liturgical leadership of his own diocese.[1] We are not staying here on the rationale for episcopacy.[2] And we may start this wholly practical chapter with four general assertions:

1. All the general principles of the leadership of worship as a pastoral and 'enabling' function of the ordained ministry apply equally forcefully to the bishop when he is officiating.[3]

2. The matter is complicated by the irregularity with which the bishop leads that particular congregation, by the existence of a (probably experienced) local leadership *in situ*, by the likely difficulty of careful joint advance planning between the bishop and the local leadership, and by other tensions which may exist between them—right through to a wholly different philosophy as to the nature of leadership in worship, or a wholly different concept of what

---

[1] For a bishop outside his own diocese see Appendix, page 56 below.

[2] There is a vast literature on this—going back of course to the early Fathers, taking a different shape amongst the Anglican Reformers—and in the generation of Hooker and Bancroft. It gets a strong political edge in the seventeenth century—whereas the new (or conceivably 'retrieved') affirmations of the Oxford Movement began from an anti-state, anti-Erastian character. The case was then built up and built (even by those busy defying the existent episcopate of the Church of England) into a semi-magical set of beliefs. This in turn made the Anglican episcopate the subject of every possible form of dispute both with Rome and with non-episcopalians, and meant that episcopal ordination was *the* great agenda item in all unity talks (a distortion of priorities which is only just being exposed today). In recent years we have seen discussion in the ARCIC Statement on ordination, in the Lima document, and in a continuing series of books, such as Peter Moore (ed.) *Bishops—Of what kind?* (SPCK, 1982), John Halliburton *The Authority of the Bishop* (SPCK, 1987), Stephen Sykes (ed.) *Authority in the Anglican Communion* (Anglican Book Centre, Toronto, 1987), and even in passing in the sad little Church of England Faith and Order Advisory Group report *The Priesthood of the Ordained Ministry* (BMU, Church House, London, 1986). Another whole *genre* of such discussion is arising at this very moment concerning the propriety of making women bishops. Most of these discussions touch on the necessity or otherwise of an undoubtedly 'valid' episcopate for secure patterns of ordination. Some of them touch the pastoral office of bishop also. But none seem to touch on his (or her) liturgical ministry at any depth—and the reverse is also true. It is not necessary to have got the full doctrine of episcopacy in relation to ecclesiology right for a bishop to get stuck into the daily demands of liturgical practice. He should simply be aware that a very 'high' concept of the bishop's office and even his person has lain behind much of the liturgical innovation and/or plagiarism of the last hundred years, and he may well start with an inbuilt mistrust of it. To put the matter at it most fully paradoxical—there is no need to have a sharp-edged doctrine or clear biblical precedent for one's post to function perfectly well as an archdeacon, or missionary society secretary, or college principal: and the same goes for being a bishop. The task is that of being a chief pastor, and, as with these other cases, any sensible occupant of the office recognizes the task and gets on with it.

[3] I have written a Grove Booklet on this—Worship Series no. 77, *Leading Worship* (1981, 1987). In this I labour the point that the leadership of worship is a *pastoral* function expressing a pastoral (and thus organic) relationship between leader and led.

this particular worship event ought to *be*. (Equally, it will be simplified by a good personal relationship—even a 'gut' relationship—of local pastors (not to mention musicians and other subsidiary leaders) with the bishop.)

3. Nevertheless, it is imperative to decide at the outset *who* is actually presiding or officiating. It does not invariably have to be the bishop simply on the grounds that he is *there*, but he should know whether or not he is fitting into a liturgy someone else is leading, or whether he is in fact the leader, responsible both for the overall conduct of the event and for any delegating of tasks.

4. The presence of the bishop is *not* a reason for extra pomp, extra formalism, extra stiff or senseless ceremonial, or a generally archaizing style.[1] God forbid that bishops should be permanently sealed into such a role by some widespread glorified ecclesiastical 'con'—such as an over-dose of Ferguson-Davie! (But this must be qualified by the recognition that often the bishop is there because it is a big event, a special occasion, a 'once-off'—and the character of such a liturgy does make special demands upon the leadership.[2])

So we ask: what is the bishop *for*?

It has helped me to get my own mind somewhat clearer by considering cartoon roles which others seem to see the bishop as fulfilling. I set these out in order to pull in and straighten the borders of the path, so that the bishop may tread more unerringly.

---

[1] What then of the mitre? Firstly, it is an extraordinarily recent development amongst Anglicans—the first English bishop to wear it is said to have been Edward King (Bishop of Lincoln, 1885-1910); and the first Archbishop of Canterbury to do so was Lang in 1929—well within living memory. Secondly, whatever symbolism (e.g. of the flames of the Spirit) the mitre has been supposed to convey, there is no popular *doctrinal* understanding of it—only a kind of folk reaction that a bishop ought to *look* out of this world. Thirdly, there is no liturgical *use* for it, and a bishop who does have to wear it should confine its use to processions. Fourthly, I have watched my new diocesan reduce its use simply by declining to wear a cope ('it keeps slipping'). This means that the mitre can only be requested with the chasuble, and that considerably reduces the parishes which ask the bishop to use it! And, fifthly, I should add that it becomes absurd when two or more bishops adopt hats and do things, even different things, with them during the rite.

It is quite wrong to reckon that the mitre is a 'norm' and the omission of it a departure from the norm. At the very least, it would be better to see the Anglican Communion as having a *twin* tradition, in which the bishop takes his own decision under no unfair pressure from this (short-lived!) latter-day re-importation of the mitre. And the 'twin' tradition should *not* be interpreted as providing a mitre for ordinations, but not for Evening Prayer—each of these can be approached as an open question re the use of the mitre.

So what does a bishop wear without a mitre? In some cathedral circumstances, a cope may still match the surrounds. In to-day's parishes, there is still a choice of alb (or 'cassock-alb' without a hood) and stole or of rochet and chimere and scarf—each with pectoral cross, if desired. But the case for even less distinctive wear is upon us.

[2] For a consideration of bishops in special events, see the Appendix on pp.59-60 below.

RATIONALE

Behind much of the received tradition, there is a theory that, of all people, the bishop is the one in a pastoral relationship with *all* the faithful. He is the 'Father in God'. He is the chief pastor. He bestows the 'cure of souls' on others, whilst insisting that it is still his. This point of view seems to be eminently correct in its starting-point—a chief pastor is indeed in one sense pastor to all. But the conclusion is then often drawn that all events belong to him, all liturgies are his preserve, all leadership is his spiritual birthright. If he cannot be physically present everywhere, yet he is metaphysically present in every liturgical celebration.[1]

But there could be another way of looking at the ecclesiology behind this. Instead of beginning with the bishop, and tacking the church onto him, we could start by examining the eucharistic assembly, the liturgical 'unit' of the people of God, and by asking what makes that particular unit function and gives it resources and self-sufficiency. On current Anglican premises the answer will then be that the presbyterate is sufficient for the purpose of most liturgical leadership[2], and that a visit by the bishop is either disruptive, or a kind of bonus, or just possibly of no great significance one way or the other—and that these judgments depend not much upon the office or generally received function of the bishop, but much more upon his personal abilities in adapting to the people and the event, in giving leadership appropriate to the occasion, in teaching the word of God, and in relating pastorally to the congregation. From this starting point it is certainly going to be more important to assess the actual liturgical event and its conduct than to produce an academic theory about what is happening simply because the bishop is participating. And the assessment itself will not necessarily concentrate on that 'completing' of the liturgical picture which liturgical romantics assert is happening when the bishop is present. In any case, it is not correctness or tidiness we should be seeking, but vigour and power and profundity, and the gift of the Holy Spirit!

Here then, as a warning, are the cartoons to avoid.

Firstly, let not the bishop become simply a liturgical dictator. The clergy at least (and perhaps lay-people also in many parishes) owe it to the bishop to inform him, to advise him, to argue with him, to negotiate with him, to communicate their own vision of their own parishes to him—and to provide him with some honest 'come-back' after the event. He should have wisdom to give—but it must be blended with local experience, local wisdom, and even local eccentricity. He must be willing to learn, and to be seen to be willing.

---

[1] Part of the trouble here is that the extrapolation from the parish pastor to the chief pastor may be drawn from the wrong idea of a parish pastor. Worship is a corporate event, and planning, presenting and leading it must not be simply the responsibility of a self-sufficient ordained liturgical boss. The extrapolation has its own problems also—what is the value of this 'boss' at events from which he is physically absent? We must be careful about the metaphysics.

[2] This does of course omit the question of when he is canonically *necessary*, particularly for confirmations, or is thought *desirable*, such as on anniversaries.

Secondly, let not the bishop become a cardboard cut-out. This has always been my greatest fear. Let not the church of God get fussed about making everything *look* right—a bishop clad aright, processing aright, parked in the right places in the building, popping out at prescribed points to say the right words and to execute the right actions, and thus pleasing the organizers and the audience with a fine and well-drilled role. No, above all the bishop is a minister of the gospel and a chief pastor, and to give him mindless, closely scripted, dummy roles, and expect him just to follow them through scrupulously, is to give the wrong message to him, and the wrong message about him. One of the great problems with the previous writings on this subject is precisely their concern for exactness of action and appearance (right down to details of little fingers) without any comparable concern for the power of God in the word, the worship, and the sacramental liturgy.[1] Let bishops escape this ultramontane concern for stage-managed *minutiae*, and they may catch up to the point to which the rest of the church has so often already advanced.

Thirdly, let not be bishop be seen as a kind of magician.[2] Of course his scarcity value and his seniority mean you will get him to lay foundation stones and to open buildings. Of course his authority is involved in instituting clergy. Of course Anglicanism has some reasons (not necessarily overwhelming ones) for restricting the administration of confirmation to bishops. But not let the church of God lapse into attributing to the bishop some inherent zapping power, such that an episcopal blessing *does* something a presbyter's cannot, or episcopal confirmation bestows what presbyterial baptism cannot.[3] It is not good for bishops, let alone for the church, for them to think they bring stored up divine

---

[1] Perhaps we should extend the 'cardboard cut-out' issue and put on paper a question-mark over the whole Anglican episcopal sub-culture, whether it is being used in church or not. We note:'My Lord' and 'Your Grace' (now marvellously being removed from the scene), 'Right Reverend' (which seems more obdurate), the use of place-names of sees as surnames of bishops, the sign of the cross as part of a bishop's signature (only matched by the erstwhile signature of the illiterate), purple stock, purple cassock, even purple cape, pectoral cross (even if stuck in breast pocket of shirt), ring with purple glass (what on earth is that for?), as well as mitre (with purple skull-cap in exotic quarters), and staff—all in addition to liturgical vesture common to other clergy also. If a bishop visits a school in England, he will often find that (a) the children will have prepared for his visit by drawing a pin-man in cope and mitre, and (b) that they have a sense of being let down if he does not come in or with full-dress uniform. The sub-culture extends to the lay fans or clients of the bishop also—particularly those who bob or curtsey to him as he goes in and out of church, those who want to kiss his ring, and those more who think no event complete without the bishop uttering a benediction.

[2] This is not at this point a reference to his being dressed like a cross between a Druid and a wizard . . .

[3] This does of course raise other doctrinal points, and the relationship between baptism and confirmation is the subject of other studies—I have written on this myself in *Anglican Confirmation* (Grove Liturgical Study no. 48, 1986). In esseence baptism is a dominical sacrament, confirmation a negotiable church rite. See Appendix, pp.58-59 below.

resources within their persons independently of the word and sacraments of God which they are to minister. It is a dreadful category mistake to see the bishop as somehow a sacrament of God in his own person simply by his being present.[1] Whatever recondite symbolism we may put in the doctrine books, we do not help the liturgical event by treating the bishop as having a unique key to the riches of God.

LEADERSHIP

The corollary of all this is that a bishop, where he is officiating, must actually *lead*, not in an exclusive way, but with a definiteness and a directness which conveys the character of the worship event to the people. There is no need usually for him to have a chair mid-stage.[2] There is even less point in his having a throne virtually off-stage. But let him lead from the front, facing the people, singing the hymns, and giving a true lead. Let his ceremonial be authentic.[3] Let his mood and style fit the event planned, or even move it ahead slightly. Let him have a vision of what *this* congregation, with *these* resources, on *this* occasion, and with *this* programme, can be—and let him and the other leaders go for it.

---

[1] There may well be a focal role for the bishop in relation to the unity of the church—especially if conceived not statically but eschatologically—but no-one partakes of grace simply by having the bishop around, or by giving him special bits to say.

[2] Of course he may need to sit down at points. But the mid-stage chair is to reflect his teaching office and possibly his cognate authority—and neither are well represented by his simply *resting* or listening to the scriptures in a mid-stage position. It is even worse if half-way through a service two strong men appear to remove his seat from its symbolic place! Mid-stage sitting seems most appropriate when, say, reading the exhortation at an ordination.

[3] I have here to confess to an occasional problem I encounter with some other contributors in this symposium. In general they are trying to write in a reforming way, with a view to streaminingg the tradition, and to requiring an element of authenticity in any rationale. But at intervals an inbuilt residual defence of some existing English episcopal ways peep through (sometimes, I suspect, simply because they think episcopal ways will not easily change!), even to the point of quite bizzare explanations. I submit that it takes the most ingenious and determined addiction to mental gymnastics to conclude with Halliburton that cope and mitre are a form of claiming the world for Christ (p.18), or with Stancliffe that having each new presbyter touch one cathedral Bible is actually to charge them more authentically with being ministers of the word than the true giving of a Bible would do (p.35) or with Michael Perham—that most utterly reasonable of writers—that for a bishop to stand holding his crook like Bo-Peep when the Gospel is being read is to say something important about the Gospel or about him (p.41). Nor is there rationale (or even rubrical support in the Church of England) for an event described as 'concelebration'—though this particular oddity does not apparently need a bishop to bring it to pass, so is outside our brief. We need one final mental heave if we are to be truly free to reflect on the received traditions—so many of them borrowed from other sources as recently as within living memory.

But how can a bishop not only fit into parish liturgy but also move it forward? A bishop with ideas in liturgy (and going round 200 or more parishes should give him a few ideas, even if he cannot find much to read) should be in position to give parishes a cross-fertilization they may not otherwise get. Pastoral regulations drop good hints, of course—whether it be standing for the eucharistic prayer, or keeping the linen clean, or offering submersion to candidates for baptism, or whatever. But a bishop may also offer, on a 'once-off' basis, that which the local pastor would have difficulty in introducing himself. Whether it is modern language, or a warm Peace, or a temporarily re-ordered interior, or shedding pomp—a firmly put case for a 'once-off' trial (to suit the bishop's whim, if necessary to the public front) may well not only succeed in itself, but may also lead a congregation into reformed ways thereafter. A bishop should not throw his weight about for the sheer sake of it—but he does not have to be a card-carrying charismatic to take advantage of actual liberty given him by the particular rite he is using, or to sense the mood and instincts (perhaps even the touch of the Holy Spirit?) in a particular congregation, and relate his leadership thoughtfully to that fact. And surely a good liturgically minded chief pastor should be fully capable of the imaginative introduction into liturgy of, say, testimony, of informal or extemporary prayer, of a healing ministry, of buzz groups, of questions during sermons, of spontaneous actions and the general 'freeing-up' of worship wherever that is appropriate? All that is urged here is that a bishop should have (a) a sound liturgical instinct behind such a 'freeing up', (b) a good understanding with the local church pastors about it, and (c) the right style of leadership to effect it.[1]

PASTOR AND TEACHER

A bishop's teaching office, insofar as it is to be exercised in a liturgical context, must be related to the above. His office is traditionally more highlighted for its teaching aspects than for its liturgical presidency. The bishop's throne is the place (or at least the symbol) of teaching. The ordination rite is shot through with the charge to be an ideological champion and expositor of the faith. The guardianship of the spiritual lives of the flock is said to inhere in his own role as teacher and propounder of the gospel of Christ. The gift of the Bible at his own ordination or consecration is integral to this task given him. And he in turn must let this role emerge throughout his liturgical ministry. He leads worship as pastor to the people—and he must preach and teach as pastor also, expounding the word of God, subtly offering high standards of teaching to the local ministers, and enriching the people of God with the truths of the gospel, closely related to their own circumstances.[2] There are hints elsewhere in this volume that the

---

[1] There should, of course, be reflection and come-back to a bishop about leadership of worship. One of the worst features of a bishop's role is that he is rarely criticized objectively to his face, and so he never learns the truth. Praise and thanks do come along of course, but he never dare trust them wholly, just because he knows that people so often will not tell him the truth. Oh, for a true levelling with each other and frank speech in love!

[2] He has many other features to his teaching office, which are not in view here—including writing, journalism and the use of the media.

bishop should be sensitive to the calendar and lectionary, not only when preaching on ordinary occasions, but al;so at confirmations.[1]

This is to take the bishop extremely seriously as the chief pastor, and is to entrust him with a truly pastoral leadership of worship. It is, on the other hand, to view his role as a hundred times more important for its functional character than for its symbolic. Every rationale for episcopacy which ends up by asserting that tasks of episcope in the church should be embodied in a *Man*—i.e. in an individual person—must go on to reckon that person to have a *Personality,*And to expect that personality to be engaged in the liturgical leadership committed to him. It will be part of the shared ministry of bishop and local presbyter and congregation that they should discern between them best what gifts (or weaknesses) the particular bishop brings to his task, and that they should plan the liturgy to enable the church to take best advantage of his gifts. If he is a chief pastor by appointment, let him be a true pastor in liturgical action.

---

[1] Here I must question a suggestion that baptisms and confirmations should be simply an incidental part of parish Visitations. Certainly it is a problem if a bishop is notorious for having three standard sermons he trots out on all confirmations occasions, irrespective of the season of the year, or of any special circumstances. In general his preaching must be much more closely lectionary-related and pastorally related to the occasion. But the opposite problem also exists—I would suggest that it is almost impossible to do confirmations *en passant,* whilst ostensibly and centrally doing something else. The liturgy of confirmation will affect the whole eucharistic liturgy, and the sermon at the confirmation will outbid other themes in the preaching. So, in my judgment, if baptism and confirmation are to come as part of the programme of a larger parish visit, their own liturgical demands cannot be ignored (or trumped) by the other demands of that visit. If this means two different liturgical occasions (yes, and two different sermons), then let the visit look that in the face, and let the planners plan accordingly.

Appendix: Notes on Special Questions

Whilst this Study in general has been attempting to lay bare principles, it may be that here and there a reader would like more discussion of some particular issue which arises in connection with the bishop in liturgy, and the editor here attempts to oblige.

A. GETTING CONSECRATED AND INAUGURATED

In England, diocesan bishops are consecrated away from their actual dioceses, for legal reasons.[1] They are then later 'enthroned', and begin their public ministry. The consecration service, whilst it is technically in the hands of the archbishop, should include an element of planning or at least requesting by the candidate.[2] Candidates should also ensure that they receive Letters of Orders afterwards, which, astonishing to relate, are not invariably issued in Anglican provinces.[3]

The enthronement ceremony, whilst it occurs in the cathedral, should involve careful joint planning with the incoming bishop, and should not be simply a dean-and-chapter production. The actual negotiating of his place in the cathedral itself should be minor and preliminary, and the beginning of his public ministry in the diocese should mark the event. This may well involve recognition and acceptance by the diocese (and by representatives of other Christian Churches, and in a different way by representatives of other faiths and of secular bodies),

---

[1] Under the present (unbelievable!) English laws, it appears that a new bishop actually *becomes* legally the bishop at the 'confirmation' ceremony—and, if a man is not already consecrated, the Church of England makes haste the next day to cover up its own embarrassment by consecrating him. He has still to kiss the monarch's hands (by which he receives back from her the temporalities of the see, including (even more astonishingly) the parochial patronage which belongs to the bishop—but which lapses to the Crown during a vacancy in the see). There then follows the 'enthronement' which is virtually wholly cosmetic, and has nothing to do with actually taking up or exercising the powers of the diocesan bishop. If a man is already consecrated and is being 'translated', then he becomes legally bishop of the diocese at this 'confirmation' ceremony in London or York—far distant from his diocese, and without anyone anywhere being much aware of it. Overseas readers will have some difficulty going backwards through this time-warp.

[2] There are some interesting questions afoot as I write this, as to how fraternally assisting bishops of the Scandinavian Lutheran Churches, of the Old Catholics, and of the United Churches of North and of South India, of Pakistan and of Bangla Desh, can participate both fully and prominently and naturally in the laying on of hands.

[3] In some parts all the bishops who share in the laying on of hands then sign the Letters of Orders, which certainly makes the point that they consecrate jointly. It also re-inforces the propriety of them all attempting actually to touch the candidate.

and the reading and preaching of the word of God, and prayer and worship.[1] It is crucial that the rite gives the correct message about the nature of the new bishop and his ministry, and thus his own input into it should be determinative. There are no set rites.

Outside England, there are clear possibilities for both events to be one—for the new diocesan to be consecrated, and for the archbishop or presiding bishop (or the dean or provost) then to 'enthrone' him. Others then step back and let the new bishop begin his ministry by his presiding at the eucharist—as in Hippolytus.

Suffragans may be consecrated in or out of their dioceses. If outside, they can then be introduced by a public rite. If inside, all will happen at one go.

B. SUFFRAGAN BISHOPS[2]

The simplest approach to the role of the suffragan bishop is to assert that in the absence of his diocesan bishop he is the chief pastor present at liturgy in his diocese. Thus no variant on anything previously discussed or advised in this Study is needed when the suffragan's role is under consideration.

When the diocesan is present, the suffragan is clearly *not* the chief pastor, and, although he may have, say, his own stall in the cathedral, he has no particular liturgical *role* to fulfil by virtue of his office. There is no point in dressing him up specially either.

There have been recent attempts to include the suffragan with the diocesan in a simultaneous episcopal role, whether in order to give re-assurance to a notoriously insecure person or to exhibit a corporate episcopate is unclear. The ventures include what can only be called 'con-ordination'—where the suffragan joins with the diocesan in uttering the ordination prayer, and joins with him in the laying on of hands, not just as an assisting presbyter but in the central episcopal role, whether it is deacon's or presbyter's orders which are being conferred. The result is liturgically unsatisfactory—most such weighty prayers have been written for one voice only, and come acorss oddly from two. But it is also quite unnecessary—no bishop should somehow feel he is being de-skilled or 'put down' if he does not ordain new ministers at stated intervals.[3] Equally the 'corporateness' of diocesan episcopacy actually depends not upon a cosmetic show

---

[1] Because this *is* the beginning of his ministry, it looks desirable that he should begin with a eucharist. If he is being consecrated at that rite (as described in the next paragraph) then the eucharist will be a standard feature of his beginning his ministry. But the secular persons present on the English pattern may daunt him or his diocese from having a eucharist, and there may be something to be said for a two-part rite, perhaps before and after lunch on a Saturday (yes, or even in some cases a Sunday), in which an inaugural eucharist for the faithful is the second part.

[2] The title 'suffragan' here includes the 'assistant', the 'co-adjutor', and even the 'area' bishop, and the singular includes the plural.

[3] There are dioceses in the world where diocesan bishops themselves never get the chance to ordain. But they are not to 'feel' any less like bishops for that. Ordinaton does not exist for the sake of the ordainer, but for the church of God and thus for the candidate. The bishop's joy is an overflow of Gd's goodness to him from the event, but God forbid that he should identify his pastorate with a need to be regularly ordaining!

of liturgical Siamese twins, but upon the degree of both delegation and trust conferred upon the suffragan by the diocesan in what is in essence still a mon-episcopal system.[1]

C. LITURGICAL CHAPLAINS

Chaplains are escorts to bishops in liturgy. They may be personal assistants bought along by the bishop himself, or they may be provided locally. Equally, they may fulfil one or other (or both) of two roles: that is, they may be there simply to beef up the occasion, like outriders alongside a monarch—or there may be necessary functions for them to perform.[2] Ferguson-Davie tells us that bishops regularly need *three* chaplains.[3] I find it all unbelievable—if the usual officiant at worship does not need such attendants, neither does the bishop. A chaplain may hold books for a bishop (but a small prayer desk, music stand, or low table, will usually do this), or a chaplain may be a psychological support for a bishop (or may be there to do his thinking from him) . . . It may come down to a matter of taste and preference on the part of the bishop.

D. BAPTISM AND CONFIRMATION

The notes under this head are not so much coaching as warning. It is otiose to urge yet again that to administer confirmation the bishop should not wear his hat, should not sit on a throne, should for preference move along a rail of kneeling confirmands (rather than have them marching up to him and bowing), has no reason to carry his crook, and may well lay on only one hand (according to the provisions of his provincial rite).[4] A bishop should understand the inner structure and rationale of the initiation rites of his province and try to work 'with the grain' of the liturgical principles. To administer adult and infant baptism together helps to make public points about each. To administer adult baptism with confirmation both saves the baptism from being a hole-in-a-corner business, and poses the unanswerable question as to the purpose of having con-

---

[1] An occasional variant at ordinations is for the suffragan to ordain the deacons, and the diocesan the presbyters, all within the same rite. This has more authenticity to it, and avoids the liturgical oddities of con-ordination, but the delegation of the laying on of hands by a diocesan bishop *who is present and sitting passively* still seems pretty odd. There is a much better case for the suffragan officiating at ordinations deliberately delegated to him *entire*—and there are some interesting questions about the way in which one candidate may be made deacon in his cathedral, and later be made presbyter in his area (or parish), with a kindred question as to what division of roles this implies for diocesan and suffragan bishops.

[2] This is similar to the question of the need of servers, cross-bearers etc. They may be there to add to the pomp and ceremony of a liturgical occasion, or they may be there because a clear liturgical function calls for them. There is always a risk of inventing tasks under the latter heading in order covertly to pursue the former aim.

[3] Ferguson-Davie, *op. cit.,* p.40.

[4] Nor is there theological reason to give oil much or any status.

firmation at all for those baptized as adults.[1] Prophetically, the new Canadian *Book of Alternative Services* (1985) has taken the logical (and biblical) step and abolished confirmation in such a case.

When a bishop is administering baptism, he may well find that a procession to a font or baptistry 'goes well', and that threefold submersion of candidates (which is the first option in the Anglican rubrics in many cases) is a joy to the recipients and genuinely powerful for the congregation.

It is impossible, *pace* David Stancliffe above, to contemplate the candidates in many Anglican dioceses ever finding their way with their supporters to a far-distant diocesan cathedral for baptism and confirmation, and sheer pastoral sense must prevail here. Nor should anyone despise celebrations with small numbers of candidates—they have a better 'flow' within the rite; they require the candidates to be seen and to speak up in a more public and demanding way; and they give the bishop a much better chance of being able to speak to each one individually (about his or her conversion or whatever) before or after the rite.

Anglicans are in the odd position of insisting, alone amongst all the Churches of Christendom, that confirmation must be administered by a bishop (though it looks as though Roman Catholic or South Indian confirmation administered by a presbyter of one of those churches would be accepted *as* confirmation when people are joining the Anglican Churches). There is a strong case for pursuing the trail blazed in America and Canada of having a rite not unlike confirmation for renewing baptismal vows, and also one for receiving not only Roman Catholics but also baptized and communicant non-episcopalians.[2]

Bishops may well look hard also at the question of admission to communion of the baptized from the point of their baptism (even in infancy)—a move which gives new directions to the rite of confirmation.[3]

E. SPECIAL EVENTS

What no book can provide in detail is a guide to all the special liturgical events of a bishop's ministry. A list, not all of which would be accepted by every bishop, might include:

---

[1] I have in the past advocated that adult baptism need not wait for the bishop to come to administer confirmation (see my Grove Worship Series no 91, *Adult Baptisms*, 1985). Now that I administer confirmation I can sense the richness as drama of a rite which includes baptisms, but the theological oddity remains whichever way adult baptism and confirmation are joined or separated.

[2] I have elsewhere set out experimental patterns for renewing baptismal vows *in water*— indeed with submersion.

[3] In my *Anglican Confirmation (op. cit.)* I point out that, if the admission to communion of youngish baptized infants comes generally to pass, then it will change the nature of confirmation. See also the Knaresborough report, *Communion before Confirmaton?* (Church House Publishing, 1985) pp.46-47. This has of course already happened in some Provinces. See also Colin Buchanan (ed.) *Nurturing Children in Communion: Essays from the Boston Consultation* (Grove Liturgical Study no. 44, 1985).

Ecumenical confirmations/visitations/inaugurations
Anniversaries of buildings/parishes/ordinations
Consecrations of sites/buildings/graveyards etc.
Inauguration of every conceivable kind of ministry
Termination or farewells ditto
Burial of urns/ashes/relics/memento caskets
Pilgrimages/processions/marches
Blessings of candles/cribs/cottages/chip shops
Liturgy surrounding drama/poetry/cultural evenings/banquets
Prayers at Council meetings/exchange visits to twin towns/naval occasions/
Masonic Lodges
Worship at Conferences/Quiet Days/Retreats

And so the list could go on. Even Ferguson-Davie could hardly provide for the lot. The sole advice here is that a bishop should continue *thinking*, should not fall for the more bizarre roles offered him, and should if possible take a creative initiative and help shape the liturgy so that it teaches and inspires—and enables him in his ministry of word (for everything in the list above requires an address!) and his liturgical leadership to teach and inspire also.

F. IUS LITURGICUM

Ius Liturgicum is an elusive concept, usually invoked in Anglicanism either when a bishop wants to do something unlawful, or some other cleric wants the bishop's connivance at something unlawful. In the Church of England itself the concept flourished—almost to the point of crowding out all other concepts of *ius*—in the years from 1928 to 1966, as a direct consequence of the bishops themselves claiming authority higher than Parliament on the one hand, and raking up every tiny precedent for the bishop *being* the law on the other.[1] This was all eliminated in the Prayer Book (Alternative and Other Services) Measure 1965 and its successor, the Church of England (Worship and Doctrine) Meausre 1974. The major power given to bishops in the sixteenth and seventeenth centuries was that of 'appeasing doubts' and settling conflicts. This may leave fuzziness, but it is a far cry from making law as you go along. Indeed, as with others, so with bishops, it is, in this writer's opinion, better to make a plain statement that one is deliberately breaking the law (presumably for some self-evidently good pastoral reason) than to pretend to hold all the powers of law within oneself.[2] Other Provinces may have different provision.

---

[1] That onto which folk latched—a remark of Archbishop Davidson before the Royal Commission on Ecclesiastical Discipline of 1904-6—will not bear this meaning. See my *Recent Liturgical Revision in the Church of England down to 1973* (Grove Booklet on Ministry and Worship no. 14, 1973 and 1984) p.5 footnote 2.

[2] This concept that the bishop has powers inherent in his person and office has crept back in the Church of England with the current oddities we have about admitting unconfirmed children to communion. It is still technically illegal, but bishops 'authorize' or 'permit' what are called 'experiments' in many places.

G. A BISHOP OUTSIDE HIS OWN DIOCESE

A bishop outside his own diocese is not a chief pastor to the local congregation (unless, on a highly speculative doctrine he has been borrowed to stand in for the local diocesan—e.g. as when taking a confirmaton service in place of him). Otherwise he is a visiting preacher or guest president of the eucharist. It is difficult to conceive what, as a bishop in the church of God at large, he should do which is different from what any other guest would do. We must beware of 'pontifical' events which stem simply from the orders of the minister officiating and have nothing to do with the ecclesial context. Certainly let not the president of the eucharist, expect the itinerant bishop, who is about to preach at the eucharist to intervene with an absolution, simply because the congregation has an exalted view of bishops in the church.

H. A BISHOP'S HOME BASE

There are two liturgical points which bear upon this:

Firstly, a bishop needs to be part of a community—it may be his family, himself with his chaplain, an extended household of some sort, or even a base within his cathedral (if he lives beside it), or within his local parish. These are the people with whom he prays (whether in his own chapel or not) on a rhythmic if not daily basis. Without them he is in a desperately lonely and exposed position.

There are of course ways in which further supporting contexts can be provided—staff meeting prayers (including eucharist), quiet days with colleagues or cells, and the (all too rare) sheer attendance at public worship. Parishes pray for their bishops daily or weekly, and that gives each bishop some stretched out helping hand from the parishes, in which, if he asks for more, astonishing generosity may always emerge. In the English situation, may there not be a case for a 'bishop's prayer meeting' once a month at the heart of a conurbation, a point where a fairly free liturgical frame would enable him and his staff to share, with anyone who would come, the needs of both diocese and city, and the needs could then be brought to God in a context of liturgical prayer and worship—and sometimes of sacrament?

Secondly, however, there is a warning. Part of the community aspect of the bishop's less public participation in worship is that *he must not be always the leader.* He has his own need to be in corporate worship where others are responsible for its conduct, and he is not. It is psychologically, theologically and spiritually wrong for him always to be cast as the great provider.

1987 TITLES

1. **(LS 49) Daily and Weekly Worship—from Jewish to Christian**
   by R. T. Beckwith, Warden of Latimer House, Oxford
   [OUT OF STOCK UNTIL REPRINTED]

2. **(LS 50) The Canons of Hippolytus**
   edited by Paul Bradshaw, Professor of Liturgics, University of Notre Dame
   These Canons, only available in manuscript in Arabic, reflect a Greek original which has been variously dated by scholars, but is here located in the early fourth century. This makes it the earliest source of Hippolytus himself.

3. **(LS 51) Modern Anglican Ordination Rites**
   edited by Colin Buchanan, Bishop of Aston
   The revisions of the last 15 years throughout the Anglican Communion are collected and presented by Colin Buchanan, who has here done for ordination rites what he has done three times in the last decades for eucharistic rites.

4. **(LS 52) Models of Liturgical Theology**
   by James Empereur, of the Jesuit School of Theology, Berkeley
   Worship may be characterized differently, depending on the dominant model at work, such as liturgy as institution, as mystery, as sacrament, as proclamation, as process, as therapeutic, and as liberation. No one model exhausts the meaning of the liturgy; no one model can be omitted from an adequate theological understanding of the worship of the assembly.

NEW—1988 TITLES

5. **(LS 53) Liturgical Formation of the Laity: The Brixen Essays**
   edited by Thomas Talley, Professor of Liturgics, General Theological Seminary, New York.
   This volume is a thoroughly edited collection of the salient papers read at the second international Anglican Liturgical Consultation held at Brixen in Northern Italy in August 1987—and, from America, Britain, and Africa alike, they combine planning aspects of the liturgy to-day in Anglicanism with the 'results' in terms of the building up of the laity.

6. **(LS 54) The Bishop in Liturgy: an Anglican Study**
   edited by Colin Buchanan, Bishop of Aston
   This symposium begins from a paper of Colin Buchanan, delivered at the Brixen Consultation but deliberately excluded from Study no. 5 summarized above. Some treatment of history, of pastoral considerations, and of expectations varying from diocese to diocese and continent to continent, leads on into practical help for bishops and for all those who welcome bishops to minister in their parishes or larger contexts. (Published in time for the Lambeth Conference.)

7. **(LS 55) Enculturation of the Liturgy** (September 1988)
   by Phillip Tovey, research student, previously tutor in liturgy in Uganda
   The author draws upon broad study and also his own experience in Africa and in Britain to pose the questions and point in a healthful direction for answers, concerning the relating of liturgy to local culture in different parts of the world.

8. **(LS 56) Essays in Early Eastern Initiation** (December 1988)
   edited by Paul Bradshaw, Professor of Liturgics, University of Notre Dame
   A well-known editor from the Church of England, a professor at Notre Dame University, presents three authors who open up new issues and provide new theories in relation to the early Eastern baptismal rites.

Alcuin Club membership is open to all applicants sending £7 (or US$18) to the Alcuin Club, Norton Vicarage, Windmill Hill, Runcorn, Cheshire WA7 6QE. Those who have previously obtained Grove Liturgical Studies on standing order will find it cheaper to join the Alcuin Club (though payment must then be made in advance, rather than arrears), but must notify Grove Books Ltd. at the same time of the cancellation of their Standing Order (or that part of it), or they may be held liable for both.

Grove Liturgical Studies

This series began in March 1975, and has been published quarterly. Nos. 1, 3-6 and 10 are out of print. Asterisked numbers have been reprinted. Prices in 1988, £2.

For full list of other 'Worship' titles and *News of Liturgy* (monthly) write to Grove Books Ltd.

THE ALCUIN CLUB and
GROUP FOR RENEWAL OF WORSHIP (GROW)

The Alcuin Club exists to promote the study of Christian liturgy in general, and in particular the liturgies of the Anglican Communion. Since its inception and foundation in 1897 it has published over 120 books and pamphlets. Members of the Club receive publications of the current year *gratis*. The Club has traditionally produced one major work of liturgical scholarship every year, and its productions have been published by traditional publishers. That pattern was completed with the 1986 publication (see below), and the Joint Editorial Board with G-R-O-W now publishes four 48-page Studies per annum through Grove Books Ltd.

Recent Alcuin titles (obtainable through booksellers, or via Grove Books Limited, post-free). (Some backnumbers are obtainable from the Alcuin Club at reduced prices.)

1980 *The Communion of Saints* (by Michael Perham) S.P.C.K. £6.95

1981 *Daily Prayer in the Early Church* (by Paul Bradshaw) S.P.C.K. £6.95

1982 *Nuptial Blessing* (by Kenneth Stevenson) S.P.C.K. £10.50

1983 *The Godly Order* (by Geoffrey Cuming) S.P.C.K. £8.50

1984 *Latest Anglican Liturgies 1976-1984* (edited by Colin Buchanan) S.P.C.K. (hardback) £25

1985 *The Meaning of Baptism* (by Raymond Burnish) S.P.C.K. £10.50

1986 *Earth and Altar* (by Donald Gray) Canterbury Press £10.50

Also 'Alcuin Club Manuals'

No. 1 *The Eucharist* (by Michael Perham) S.P.C.K. 1981, £2.25

No. 3 *Family Services* (by Kenneth Stevenson) S.P.C.K. 1981, £2.25

The Group for Renewal Of Worship—'GROW' has been responsible since 1971 for the Grove Booklets on Ministry and Worship (now the Grove Worship Series), and since 1975 for the quarterly scholarly 'Grove Liturgical Studies' to which the new joint Alcuin/GROW Studies stand in straight succession. Backnumbers from the twelve years of publication are available at £2 (or $4.50 via USA importers) from Grove Books Ltd., or via booksellers. See list overleaf.